$7.95

DINING IN—HOUSTON
VOL. II

PEANUT BUTTER PUBLISHING   SEATTLE, WASHINGTON

DINING IN—HOUSTON VOL. II

By Ann Criswell
Foreword by Joanne King Herring

PEANUT BUTTER PUBLISHING
2733 4th Avenue South   Seattle, Washington 98134

Cover photo: Budd Seslar/Photography

Second printing September 1981

CONTENTS

Foreword   *vii*
About the Author   *ix*
Brennan's   1
Charley's 517   11
Che   17
China Garden   25
Confederate House   35
D'Amico's   43
Foulard's   53
The Good Eats Cafe   63
Hugo's Window Box   71
La Quiche   77
Maxim's   87
Ninfa's   93
Nino's   101
Rainbow Lodge   109
The Rivoli   117
Rotisserie for Beef and Bird   123
Rudi's   131
Ruggle's   139
Tivoli Inn   145
Tony's   151
Uncle Tai's   159
Index   *171*

FOREWORD

There isn't an animal living that doesn't like to eat. When it comes right down to it, eating is the only one of the seven deadly sins you can really enjoy all by yourself. Of course, it's much more fun to enjoy it with people you love. That's why dining out is immediately a party—with you as guest of honor.

My great aunt, the only "grandmother" I ever knew, thought nothing of having a sit-down dinner for eighty. Everybody in the immediate family was expected to help. Thus I grew up appreciating what it takes to produce a successful dinner. It's a four letter word, W-O-R-K! DINING IN—HOUSTON has made it a lot easier and a lot more fun. From this one volume you can learn where to eat out and what to eat in.

Those of us who grew up in Houston know that for many years Houston was almost a city behind walls; if you didn't know someone to invite you home for dinner, it wasn't much fun. Good food could be found in a few clubs and restaurants, but most of the elegance, tradition and appreciation of fine food was to be found at home. Today there is such a wide variety of choices that one can be transported to China, France, early Texas, Mexico, Japan or fifteenth century England within minutes of home. A lively topic of conversation among Houstonians is the latest bistro or other new mecca of epicurean splendor. Texans are using and appreciating their fine restaurants.

As the honorary consul for Pakistan and the Kingdom of Morocco, I have entertained many official guests and foreign dignitaries. They loved having real grass-roots Texas food. We served omelets filled with Texas crabmeat to the King of Sweden and gave the King of Jordan's entourage shrimp, steak and homemade peach ice cream. The prime minister of Belgium was somewhat dismayed by the Tex-Mex hors d'oeuvres but enchanted by the quail on toast.

We do have a cuisine: a combination of Old South, Tex-Mex and hearty ranch cooking. It is memorable, and it is good! Tex-Mex is a unique blend of Mexican and Texan cooking. It is not for the faint-hearted, but is beloved by Texans. Texas steaks, coupled with baked potatoes stuffed with sour cream, cheese, chives and other goodies, are a national treasure. Our crabmeat, shrimp, oysters and other seafood could make a Lorelei purr. Quail, cabrito (roast young kid goat), fried chicken with cream gravy, corn bread, pecan pie, iced tea with orange juice and mint reflect our heritage.

With the glorious restaurants of Houston spread out before you like the contents of Ali Baba's cave, it would be a shame to miss one of them. Their kindness in sharing their best with you in this cookbook is pure delight. You can enjoy your favorite dishes at a restaurant and later duplicate many of them at home. And what a wonderful souvenir with which to remember the restaurants and your visit to Houston, if you don't live here.

To utilize the cookbook to the fullest, regularly plan a special dinner out with friends every week or so at a different restaurant using the cookbook as a travelogue.

Magic is everywhere; we just have to capture it to make it ours. This enchanting book can be your magic wand. Besides, it's fun to read.

Joanne King Herring

ABOUT THE AUTHOR

Ann Criswell, who has been at the Houston Chronicle since 1961, has been food editor since 1966. An enthusiastic cook, food and wine writer, she has traveled in Europe and judged several national food contests. Ann is the co-author of the first volume of *"Dining In— Houston,"* has edited "Cooking Collectibles" (the sales from which benefit the Houston Chapter of the American Cancer Society) and written magazine food stories.

Brennan's

Dinner for Six

Crawfish Etouffée in Pastry

Cream of Fresh Spinach Soup

Chatelaine Salad

Filet Mignon Debris

Crêpes Fitzgerald

Cafe Brûlot

Wine:

With Etouffée, Soup and Salad—Grand Vendiers Vouvray
With Filet Mignon—Simi Cabernet Sauvignon

Ella, Adelaide, Dick and John Brennan, Owners
Noel Hennebery, General Manager
David Grice, Chef

Along with their distinctive French-Creole cuisine, the Brennan family brought a generous helping of New Orleans tradition to Houston. Thirteen years ago the restaurant took over the former Junior League Building, a landmark designed by John Staub, a renowned Houston architect. The Brennans asked New Orleans architect August Perez to give the restaurant a New Orleans character, which he did by designing cool, shaded brick walkways, distinctive woodwork and paneling and French doors opening onto a lush patio centered by a splashing fountain. The Brennan family gave it a homelike atmosphere with fabric-covered walls and matching draperies, antiques, crisp linens, fresh flower arrangements and a white lattice garden room—the Belle Terrace—upstairs.

Brennan's quickly became (and has remained) a gathering spot for Houstonians on special occasions such as birthdays and anniversaries. Thousands have made breakfast at Brennan's, cocktails, and the Dixieland Jazz Brunch their own cherished traditions. The Wine Room, which boasts one of the finest cellars in the city, is popular for private parties and small luncheons and receptions. Chef Paul Prudhomme of New Orleans initiated a new Brennan's event, the First of the Season, a celebration of seasonal bounty such as crawfish, scrod from Boston, fennel from California, fresh fruits and berries and shad roe.

At Brennan's you find the hallmarks of Louisiana cuisine—gumbo, shrimp and oysters, pecan and praline dishes, Creole sauces, Café Brulot and Bananas Foster, which Brennan's introduced to the world. They are on the menu alongside sophisticated international veal dishes, Beef Wellington and Crêpes Suzette, and dishes created and named for friends such as Crêpe Welch, named for Houston attorney Robert Welch, and Jill Jackson Salad, named for a newspaper columnist in New Orleans.

3300 Smith Street

CRAWFISH ETOUFFEE IN PASTRY SHELLS

2 large onions, minced
1 rib celery, minced
1 large bell pepper, minced
2 cloves garlic, minced
¼ pound butter
1 to 2 tablespoons flour
3 pounds crawfish tails and fat
½ cup chopped green onion
¼ cup chopped fresh parsley
Salt, red and black pepper to taste
1 cup water
6 baked pastry shells

1. Using a large saucepan, sauté minced vegetables and garlic in melted butter over low heat until wilted and transparent. Stir in flour.
2. Add crawfish tails and fat, green onions and parsley. Season to taste with salt and 2 peppers.
3. Add hot water (may need more or less according to desired thickness of gravy). Let simmer in a covered pot until tails are tender.
4. Serve in pastry shells.

Crawfish is available fresh during the season but may be found frozen in some fish markets and fine food stores. The crawfish fat helps provide full flavor. Shrimp or lobster may be substituted if crawfish is not available.

CREAM OF SPINACH SOUP

1 pound fresh spinach
¼ pound butter
½ cup minced onion
1 clove garlic, crushed and chopped
4 ounces flour (about 1 cup)
3 chicken bouillon cubes dissolved in 1 pint water
Salt and pepper to taste
2 tablespoons Worcestershire sauce
1 pint half-and-half
½ cup dry sherry

1. Wash spinach, remove stems and chop. Sauté in butter with onion and garlic.
2. Add flour, stirring well, and cook on low temperature 5 minutes, stirring frequently with a whisk.
3. Add chicken stock, salt and pepper and stir.
4. Bring to a boil. Simmer 10 minutes or until flour has blended well with sauce and there are no lumps. Add Worcestershire sauce.
5. Over low heat, add half-and-half, stirring slowly until hot. Add sherry, heat a few minutes and serve.

CHATELAINE SALAD

3 bunches fresh watercress
3 hard-cooked eggs, diced
1 can (about 14 ounces) artichoke hearts, drained
¼ cup chopped pimiento
Bottled sharp French dressing

1. Clean and wash watercress. Pat dry.
2. Cut artichoke hearts in quarters.
3. Mix all ingredients in bowl, adding dressing to taste. Toss gently so watercress is not bruised.
4. Serve on chilled plates.

FILET MIGNON DEBRIS

*Debris is a new haute Creole sauce of the crispy outside crumbles
of roast beef simmered in a rich stock. You must have a very heavy,
very large roasting pan which can withstand 2 hours at 500 degrees,
such as those used by restaurants, or the mixture may damage the pan
or smoke up the kitchen. Your own stock and bottled brown sauce
found in gourmet departments may be substituted for these stock and
brown sauce recipes.*

6 (8-ounce) filets mignon
Creole seasoning
Beef bones, broken into 1-inch chunks
1 cup diced celery
1 cup diced onion
1 cup diced green pepper
1 cup diced carrot
1 cup chopped green onion (tops and bottoms)
2½ cups rich, thick **Brown Sauce**
2½ cups **Beef Stock** or water
6 ounces small cubes or ground steak trimmings with fat
   (from butcher shop if necessary)
¼ cup red wine
½ ounce Cognac or brandy
Holland Rusk biscuits

1. Season filets to taste with Creole seasoning. Preheat oven to
   500 degrees.
2. To make the Debris Sauce: In very large, very heavy roasting pan
   coated with non-stick spray, combine bones, celery, onion, green
   pepper, carrot and green onion; sprinkle with Creole seasoning.
   Roast in oven 2 hours at 500 degrees. Mixture should burn very
   much during this roasting time, and when finished, all ingredients
   will be very black. Stir occasionally while in oven.
3. Remove from oven and stir to loosen burnt pieces. Pour **Brown
   Sauce** and **Beef Stock** over Debris Sauce. Mix well.
4. Reduce oven temperature to 350 degrees and return pan to
   oven 1 hour.
5. While sauce is finishing, put steak trimmings, which have been well
   seasoned with Creole seasoning, in oven separately. Let cook until
   very dry, crunchy and crumbly to the touch.
6. Broil or pan-broil filets in a heavy cast iron skillet to desired
   doneness. (May be barbecued.)

7. Remove Debris Sauce from oven and strain through a very fine strainer. Bring strained mixture to a boil in a small saucepan. If it does not thicken to the consistency of whipping cream, thicken it with a roux made by mixing 1 tablespoon oil and 1½ tablespoons flour in a small bowl. Stir while pouring roux into mixture. Stir steak trimmings into simmering sauce. Bring the sauce back to boil and stir in wine and brandy. Arrange filets over Holland Rusk biscuits and pour the sauce over.

Beef Stock

2 (4-inch) beef marrow bones
3 full rib bones, broken
2 quarts water
4 ounces stew meat
2 medium onions, halved, with 2 whole cloves stuck in each half
3 ribs celery, chopped
3 medium carrots, split
4 bay leaves
½ bunch parsley, washed and chopped

1. Brown beef marrow bones and rib bones in oven.
2. In a 1-gallon saucepot over high heat, add water and browned bones, then stew meat, onions, celery, carrots, bay leaves and parsley. Bring to a rapid boil. Immediately turn heat down to a slow simmer and cook at least 2 hours, preferably 4.
3. As water evaporates, add more to keep level at about 2 quarts.

Beef Brown Sauce

¾ tablespoon oil and 1½ tablespoons flour for roux
2 cups **Beef Stock**
½ cup chopped onion
1 teaspoon Worcestershire sauce
1 tablespoon tomato purée
1 bay leaf
Small pinch of oregano
Small pinch of granulated garlic
Black pepper, cayenne and salt to taste
2 tablespoons Burgundy wine

1. Heat oil to 300 degrees in a small saucepan over medium heat. Stir in flour all at once and blend well, stirring constantly, about 5 minutes or until roux is red brown. Remove from heat and set aside.
2. In large pot, bring beef stock to a boil over moderate heat. Add onion, Worcestershire, tomato purée, bay leaf, oregano, garlic, cayenne, black pepper and salt. Reduce heat and simmer 1 to 1¼ hours, stirring occasionally.
3. Add roux, blend in well and simmer 30 minutes. Remove from heat and add wine. Makes 1 cup.

Creole seasoning can be found packaged in the spice shelves of some markets. If not available, make your own or substitute a mixture of salt, garlic powder, black pepper, cayenne and cumin or chili powder.

CREPES FITZGERALD

1 (8-ounce) package cream cheese, softened
12 tablespoons sour cream
12 crêpes
3 cups strawberries
Sugar to taste
1 tablespoon butter
Strawberry liqueur
Kirsch (clear cherry brandy)

1. Prepare Crêpes and keep warm in a towel.
2. Roll cream cheese and sour cream (2 heaping teaspoons cream cheese and 2 tablespoons sour cream per crêpe) in crêpes and place on plate.
3. In a chafing dish, cook strawberries in sugar and a little melted butter. If using fresh berries, sweeten to taste and use berries with juice. If using frozen berries, less sugar will be needed.
4. Warm a ladle of strawberry liqueur and kirsch, light it with a long match and flame liqueur. Pour over crêpes.

Crêpes

2 eggs
¾ cup sifted flour
1 teaspoon sugar
Pinch of salt
Milk

1. Mix eggs with flour, sugar and salt.
2. Add milk until batter is the consistency of condensed milk. Beat until smooth.
3. Heat a 6-inch skillet which has been oiled with a pastry brush dipped in vegetable oil. Pour 2 tablespoons batter into pan, tilting quickly to distribute batter evenly. Cook 1 minute or so, just until brown, then turn and brown other side. Oil pan with brush and repeat for all crêpes. Keep warm.
4. Use 2 crêpes per serving.

CAFE BRULOT

1 (4-inch) cinnamon stick
12 whole cloves
Peel of 2 oranges, cut in thin slivers
Peel of 2 lemons, cut in thin slivers
6 sugar lumps
8 ounces brandy
2 ounces Curaçao
1 quart strong, black coffee

1. In a brûlot bowl or chafing dish, mash cinnamon, cloves, orange peel, lemon peel and sugar lumps with a ladle.
2. Add brandy and Curaçao and stir to combine.
3. Carefully ignite brandy and mix until sugar is dissolved.
4. Gradually add coffee and continue mixing until flame flickers out.
5. Serve hot in brûlot cups or demitasses. Makes 10 to 12 servings.

Charley's 517

Dinner for Six

Oysters Bourguignon

Vichyssoise with Walnuts

Snapper Pontchartrain

Carrots Lyonnaise

Swedish Cream with Fresh Raspberries

Wine:

*With Oysters and Soup—Robert Mondavi Fumé Blanc
1978
With Snapper—Dupleix Saint-Veran 1978
After Dinner—Coffee and Port, Fonseca Bin 27*

*J. William Sharman Jr., Owner
Karl Goedereis, Manager
Curtis Calhoun, Chef*

Charley's 517 blends a little of New York and a little of New Orleans in an atmospheric downtown restaurant that serves the business trade at lunch and the candlelight-and-wine set at dinner. Its proximity to the Nina Vance Alley Theatre, Jones Hall for the Performing Arts, Music Hall and the Civic Center contributes to its dual role as a day and night restaurant. The performing arts also gave Charley's its decorating theme for the lounge—walls are hung with framed programs from the theater, symphony, ballet, opera and musicals and historical newspaper pages. Waiters often practice their own dining room drama with tableside cooking.

Subtle lighting and decor, a mix of brick walls and arches, forest green leather, a mirrored wall and other walls hung with American impressionist paintings give the restaurant and intimate wine room an air of quiet refuge.

Charley's boasts an excellent wine list reflecting owner Bill Sharman's interest in wines. There are more than 300 wines on the printed list which includes a helpful vintage chart and rating. "We may not have as large a cellar as some restaurants, but we do have an incredible variety of wines—probably the biggest list in the city," says Julian Fertitta of Charley's.

Chef Curtis Calhoun, a Creole by birth and trained in France, is one of many staff members who helped open Charley's in 1970 and are still there. His background accounts for the New Orleans touch to the menu—gumbo, Snapper Pontchartrain (the most popular item on the menu), Pralines Kathleen and Bananas Foster.

The emphasis is on fresh food, especially seafood and fish, which is fileted in their own kitchen, says Fertitta. If it isn't available fresh, fish just isn't served, he says. They also look for special seasonally available items, such as salmon, to feature. Fertitta says they tried to make the menu unpretentious but interesting, with classic additions to the Creole fare such as roast duck, steaks, Beef Wellington, escargot and veal dishes.

517 Louisiana

OYSTERS BOURGUIGNON

36 medium oysters, shucked
¾ pound butter, melted
10 small cloves garlic
Salt and pepper
½ cup very dry sherry
½ cup brown sauce
½ cup freshly grated Parmesan cheese

1. Wash oysters in salty water. Drain.
2. Melt butter in saucepan. Add garlic and cook until garlic is tender.
3. Add oysters and cook 15 minutes over medium heat or until oysters curl.
4. Add salt and pepper, sherry and brown sauce. Cook 5 minutes.
5. Arrange oysters in casserole. Sprinkle with Parmesan and brown under broiler.

VICHYSSOISE WITH WALNUTS

At Charley's we like to serve this soup ice cold. We make it in gallon containers and usually put them in the freezer about 8 a.m. and transfer them to the refrigerator about 11 a.m. before luncheon service. If you like the soup cold, you might adopt this method at home. However, when working with a smaller amount, don't let it freeze.

½ pound butter
5 leeks (use part of green tops, too), peeled and cut up
6 medium potatoes, peeled and cut in chunks
1 onion, chopped
2 cups water
4½ cups half-and-half
Salt and pepper to taste
1 teaspoon celery salt
1 tablespoon Maggi seasoning
Finely chopped walnuts

continued

1. Melt butter in saucepan. Add leeks, potatoes and onion; sauté for 2 to 3 minutes. Add water and cook until vegetables are tender, about 15 minutes. Drain.
2. Heat half-and-half. Add 4 cups to potatoes and cook until done. Either mash or blend in blender. Strain through a very fine strainer.
3. Add salt, pepper, Maggi seasoning and remaining half-and-half.
4. Chill thoroughly in refrigerator. When ready to serve, sprinkle with finely chopped walnuts. Serve in chilled bowl with chilled spoon.

RED SNAPPER PONTCHARTRAIN

6 (6-ounce) red snapper filets
Flour
1 pint oil
½ cup softened butter
2 to 3 cloves garlic, pressed
1 cup brown sauce (see note)
¼ cup sherry
1 tablespoon lemon juice
Salt and pepper
1 tablespoon Worcestershire sauce
1 tablespoon fresh chopped parsley
1 pound lump crab meat
12 peeled, cooked shrimp

1. Wash snapper and dry. Dredge in flour.
2. Heat oil in large skillet. Brown snapper on both sides, then remove from pan and pour out oil. Set fish aside.
3. Mix butter with garlic. Melt over medium heat (don't let burn). Add brown sauce, sherry, lemon juice, salt and pepper, Worcestershire sauce and chopped parsley. Stir well.
4. Arrange snapper on plates. Heat crab and shrimp in a little butter and arrange shrimp on top of crab over snapper. Pour sauce on top.
5. If desired, garnish with a sprig of parsley and lemon wedge or cartwheel.

Note: Use recipe in this book for brown sauce (see index) or make your own. If desired, use Knorr packaged brown sauce.

CARROTS LYONNAISE

6 cups julienne carrot strips (about 1 pound carrots or 2 carrots
    per person)
2 cups sliced onion
½ pound butter, melted
2 cups water
Salt and pepper
¼ cup fresh chopped parsley

1. Add carrots and onions to butter in saucepan. Sauté 2 to 3
   minutes.
2. Add water, salt and pepper. Cook until carrots are tender. Drain.
3. Keep warm until ready to serve. Add chopped parsley, mix well
   and serve.

SWEDISH CREAM WITH FRESH RASPBERRIES

1 quart whipping cream
¼ pound powdered sugar
1 teaspoon vanilla
¼ cup Grand Marnier
1 quart fresh raspberries

1. Chill cream, bowl and beaters thoroughly. Whip cream until
   medium heavy.
2. Turn beaters on low speed and add powdered sugar, vanilla and
   liqueur. Beat 3 minutes.
3. Refrigerate until ready to serve with berries.

*This makes a wonderful sauce to serve with fresh berries or fruit
or as a sauce for desserts. It is between the consistency of pouring
cream and whipped cream and is silky smooth. A delicious variation
is to substitute amaretto for the Grand Marnier and serve with
fresh peaches.*

Dinner for Four

Oysters à l'Ancienne

Champignons de Paris

Lamb Loin Beauharnaise

Poireaux Salad

Walnut Torte

Wine:
With Oysters and Soup—Meursault 1978
With Lamb—Château Moulin des Carruades 1974
With Torte—Moët et Chandon White Star Champagne
After Dinner—Glass of Port

Michael W. Feldott, Owner
Amy Ferguson, Chef

Art deco elegance and imaginative food make Che one of the top choices of the city's cognoscenti. Located upstairs in the Plaza Hotel, near the art museums, the supper-club-style restaurant is a chic retreat of gray velvet walls, blue-sky ceilings, paintings and fresh flowers in window box profusion.

"The setting is formal, but not pretentious, and because the dining room is small—it only seats forty-eight—we try to provide personal service as well as good food," says twenty-four-year-old chef Amy Ferguson. She might be described as a culinary whiz kid. She began training in Europe as a teen-ager and her background includes a stint at the Cordon Bleu in Paris.

She believes in fresh food of the highest quality prepared with a flair. She grows fresh herbs to use at Che and emphasizes that because everything is natural the staff is prepared to cater to customers' special diet requirements and special requests. "We cut all our own meat, make our own pastries and use no artificial additives," she says.

The food marks the change of seasons at Che. In the spring, for example, Rack of Spring Lamb with Herbs might be featured, but in the summer you will find lamb chops marinated in a vinaigrette served cold. In the fall or winter, a hearty Lamb Nivernaise, double-cut lamb chops topped with prosciutto-mushroom sauce and tomato sauce, might be offered.

Some of the more unusual menu items seasonally are a smoked rainbow trout appetizer, leek salad and Roast Rack of Veal Choron ("I think we are the only restaurant here offering a rack of veal and lamb loin," says Chef Ferguson).

Che has only been open since 1977 but has earned a two-star rating from *Texas Monthly* magazine, indicating it is one of the best restaurants in the state.

5020 Montrose

OYSTERS A L'ANCIENNE

2 large green bell peppers, finely chopped
1¾ cups finely chopped fresh mushrooms
⅓ cup finely chopped shallots
1½ pounds unsalted butter
1 (3-ounce) can pimientos, drained and finely diced
20 oysters, shucked and left on the half shell
5 strips bacon, cut into 4-inch pieces

1. Sauté finely chopped vegetables, except pimiento, in 1 pound butter
   until translucent.
2. Cool mixture in an ice bath. As it cools, whisk in remaining butter,
   then stir in diced pimiento. Cooling can be done by setting bowl
   containing sautéed vegetables in a larger bowl of ice and stirring
   mixture occasionally. Or, slowly whip mixture in electric mixer.
   Do not overbeat or vegetables will be mushy.
3. Arrange oysters on the half shell on a baking sheet and top each
   with 1 tablespoon of the butter mixture.
4. Top each with a slice of bacon.
5. Bake 7 to 10 minutes in a 500-degree oven until oysters are
   shirred and bacon is cooked.

*Many people like to bake the oysters on a bed of rock salt, but then the
juices may be lost. I think it is better to use a plain baking pan so you
can retrieve the juices and spoon them over the oysters.*

*Bacon will be more crisp if you parcook it a little in the oven on a
baking sheet.*

CHAMPIGNONS DE PARIS

2 tablespoons butter
2 to 3 shallots, minced
1 pound fresh mushrooms, ground or chopped
6 cups chicken stock
Salt and pepper
1 teaspoon fresh lemon juice
1 lemon, thinly sliced

continued

1. Melt butter and sauté shallots until they are transparent.
2. Add mushrooms and cook 5 minutes, stirring occasionally.
3. Add chicken stock and bring to a full boil. Reduce heat and simmer uncovered 30 minutes.
4. Strain the soup through a coarse sieve, pressing the mushrooms firmly to extract all the liquid. The strainer must be coarse enough that some of the mushroom specks will go through.
5. Season with salt, pepper and lemon juice.
6. Garnish each soup plate or bowl with 2 lemon slices.

LAMB LOIN BEAUHARNAISE

This is fairly involved to do at home because of the several sauce components. However, you can make a large quantity of beef stock and brown sauce and freeze leftovers so you have some on hand when needed.

Ask a butcher to cut and prepare the lamb loins for you. You may have to go to a specialty meat market for this, although any butcher should be able to cut it. For the sake of tenderness and to give the suggestion of more, cut loin on the diagonal in thin slivers.

2 lamb loins, cleaned (about 3 pounds in all)
Sauce Madere
Béarnaise Sauce
Parsley

1. Prepare **Sauce Madere** and **Béarnaise Sauce**.
2. Preheat oven to 450 or 500 degrees.
3. About 20 minutes before serving time, sear the lamb loins and then roast in an open roasting pan to desired doneness, about 10 to 15 minutes. Remove from oven, arrange in serving dish and cover with ⅔ of the **Sauce Madere**.
4. Add the remaining **Sauce Madere** to the **Béarnaise Sauce** to make **Beauharnaise Sauce** and pour a strip atop the **Sauce Madere** on the lamb.
5. Garnish with parsley and serve.

Sauce Madere

2 teaspoons minced shallots
½ cup Madeira wine
2 cups *Brown Sauce*
2 tablespoons *Tarragon Butter*
Salt

1. Combine the shallots and the wine and boil until reduced by half.
2. Add *Brown Sauce* and cook 2 to 3 minutes. Whip in the *Tarragon Butter* and cook another minute.
3. Season with salt and a hint of Madeira to enhance the flavor.

Brown Sauce

¼ cup clarified butter
¼ cup diced ham
½ cup chopped onions
¼ cup chopped carrots
¼ cup flour
4 cups hot beef stock
1 cup tomato paste
Bouquet garni

1. Melt butter in a saucepan and add ham, onions and carrots. When vegetables are golden, add flour and cook, stirring, until well browned.
2. Slowly add stock, stirring constantly until smooth and thickened.
3. Add tomato paste and bouquet garni, mixing well; simmer until reduced by about half. Stir occasionally and skim off any fat that forms on the top. Strain sauce before using.

Tarragon Butter

¼ pound unsalted butter
2 tablespoons dried tarragon
1 tablespoon minced shallots

Combine all ingredients and blend well. (Leftover butter may be used for seasoning other dishes.)

Béarnaise Sauce

3 egg yolks at room temperature
1 cup clarified butter at room temperature
¼ cup tarragon vinegar
2 tablespoons dried tarragon
1 teaspoon chopped shallots
3 peppercorns
Salt to taste

1. Cook egg yolks in top of a double boiler over simmering water on medium heat, whipping constantly until tripled in volume.
2. Remove from heat and whip in butter, a little at a time, until all is used.
3. In a separate saucepan, combine vinegar, tarragon, shallots and peppercorns and cook until reduced by at least half.
4. Strain the reduction into the egg mixture, squeezing the tarragon to extract all the liquid. (There should only be a small amount, about 1 tablespoon.) Stir until well blended.
5. Place container in a pan of warm, not hot, water until serving time.

POIREAUX SALAD

It's best to make the salad an hour or two ahead.

8 medium leeks, cleaned (whites only)
¼ cup currants
⅓ cup tarragon vinegar
2 tablespoons French olive oil
Salt and pepper

1. Blanch leeks uncovered in boiling salted water until tender, about 10 minutes. Drain.
2. Sprinkle with currants, vinegar and oil. Season to taste with salt and pepper.
3. Allow to sit at room temperature until serving time, to season.

WALNUT TORTE
(Gateaux aux Noisettes)

⅓ pound (1½ cups) finely chopped walnuts
⅔ cup fine dry bread crumbs
¼ teaspoon salt
¼ teaspoon mace
⅛ teaspoon cloves
5 eggs at room temperature, separated
1 cup sugar
1½ teaspoons fresh lemon juice
1 teaspoon grated lemon peel
3 cups chilled whipping cream
½ cup sifted powdered sugar

1. Combine chopped walnuts, bread crumbs, salt, mace and cloves. Mix and set aside.
2. Preheat oven to 300 degrees.
3. Beat egg yolks with sugar, lemon juice and peel 3 minutes at medium speed of electric mixer. Blend into nut mixture.
4. Beat egg whites in small deep bowl until rounded peaks are formed. Fold into batter.
5. Butter the bottom of a 9x5x3-inch loaf pan, preferably a glass bread pan. Line the bottom with wax paper cut to fit exactly. Butter the wax paper.
6. Pour in the batter and bake 60 to 65 minutes. Let cool 2 minutes before removing from pan. Wrap in wax paper and let sit overnight.
7. Next day, slice cake in 4 horizontal layers. Fill between layers and cover top with Crème Chantilly made by whipping cream and powdered sugar. To serve, cut in ½-inch thick slices.

Instead of bread crumbs, finely crushed plain cookies or cake (such as genoise) may be used.

Be sure bowl, beaters and cream are thoroughly chilled so cream will whip properly.

A glass pan is best for the torte; metal pans seem to produce a harder crust. To cut the cake, outline each layer by scoring with a knife tip around the edge. Or, lay cake on its side and slice.

華園 CHINA GARDEN 酒家

Dinner for Six

Hot and Sour Soup

Paper-Wrapped Fried Chicken

Stir-Fried Shrimp with Garlic

Stir-Fried Beef with Oyster Sauce

Stir-Fried Chicken with Walnuts

Stir-Fried Vegetarian Dish

Wine:
Wan Fu (or White Graves) or Beer

David and Marian Jue, Owners

Since 1968, China Garden has grown from a little import shop to a 270-seat restaurant a few blocks east of the downtown mainstream. The restaurant is owned by David Jue and his wife Marian, who were born in Canton, China. Jue came to San Francisco when he was sixteen knowing no English and with only ten dollars in his pocket. After two years in San Francisco, where he learned English, he moved to Shreveport, Louisiana and worked in an uncle's Chinese-American twenty-four-hour restaurant. There he learned to cook blue plate specials, Louisiana Cajun dishes and hush puppies as well as his native Cantonese dishes.

China Garden's casual atmosphere appeals to those who like classic Cantonese dishes, including banquet foods such as whole steamed fish and duck. Jue will produce special Chinese gourmet dinners for six or more with twenty-four-hour notice. Clay pot specialty dishes typical of Canton were added after the restaurant moved to its present location in 1979.

The restaurant is mainly a family operation, but the menu also lists spicier Szechuan fare produced by China Garden's Mandarin chefs. Live lobster is a menu feature; they also make their own noodles. Many other menu listings are based on seasonal foods, such as the first spring asparagus. Its arrival is eagerly anticipated by customers who know spring is really here when Beef and Fresh Asparagus is available. Occasionally, in season, regular patrons bring in their own fresh crabs to be cooked.

An enthusiastic group of China Garden's loyal patrons have originated a Solidarity Day rally. Once a year they get together to enjoy an elaborate multi-course banquet and to toast the Jues.

The restaurant is done in rich reds with gold leaf and turquoise accents in decorative Chinese panels around the ceiling. Walls are paneled or papered in red and gold foil. Inlaid black lacquer screens, dragon plaques, framed dimensional scenes created from shells and traditional Chinese lanterns are all from Hong Kong.

1602 Leeland at Crawford

*This dinner may seem difficult because of so many stir-fried dishes.
However, it is much easier and faster if you prepare and organize all
ingredients for each dish ahead of time. Assemble everything for one
dish on a tray next to the wok or cooking area. Heat wok and be sure
it's hot before adding oil. Let oil heat to almost smoking, then quickly
stir-fry dish. Keep warm while cooking the next dish. The soup may
be made about a half an hour ahead, if desired, and kept warm until
serving time.*

HOT AND SOUR SOUP

¼ cup shredded bean curd
2 tablespoons Chinese black mushrooms, soaked in water to soften
2 tablespoons cooked shredded Chinese or smoked ham
2 ounces pork loin (cooked or uncooked)
½ cup small shrimp, peeled and deveined
2 eggs
Soy sauce
Cornstarch
Sesame oil
3 tablespoons vinegar
1 teaspoon black pepper
1 tablespoon chopped cilantro (fresh coriander or Chinese parsley)
2 tablespoons shredded green onion
2 tablespoons shredded ginger root
Water
2 teaspoons salt
1 teaspoon flavor enhancer
1 teaspoon sugar

1. Briefly blanch bean curd, softened mushrooms, ham, pork and shrimp
   in boiling water and remove. Beat eggs lightly.
2. Shred pork loin and mix with 1 teaspoon soy sauce, 1 teaspoon
   cornstarch and ½ teaspoon sesame oil.
3. Place 2 tablespoons soy sauce, 1 teaspoon sesame oil, the vinegar,
   pepper, cilantro, green onion and ginger root in a large soup bowl.
4. Heat 6 cups water, salt, flavor enhancer and sugar to boiling. Add
   bean curd, mushrooms and ham; when liquid boils again, add shredded
   pork and shrimp. Stir to separate pork shreds. Dissolve 3 tablespoons
   cornstarch in 3 tablespoons water and stir in to thicken.
5. Turn off heat and add eggs slowly in a thin stream; stir lightly and
   pour into soup bowl. Mix and serve, ladling out into individual bowls.

PAPER-WRAPPED FRIED CHICKEN

²/₃ pound boneless chicken
1 teaspoon salt
½ teaspoon sugar
1 teaspoon rice wine
¼ teaspoon flavor enhancer
16 shreds hot fresh red peppers
16 sprigs cilantro
6 cups oil
16 pieces heavy duty cellophane, cut into 4-inch squares

1. Slice chicken in 16 paper-thin pieces. Mix with salt, sugar, rice wine and flavor enhancer and let marinate 20 minutes.
2. On each square of cellophane, place 1 shred hot pepper, 1 sprig cilantro and 1 piece chicken. Wrap securely to form little packages as you would wrap egg rolls: fold one corner toward the opposite corner over filling. Fold left side, then the right side, toward the middle, overlapping each other. Fold bottom squared edge up to form a rectangle (similar to an envelope) with triangular flap on top. Fold over the remaining corner and press down envelope-style. Dab a little water on flap to hold if necessary.
3. Heat oil and deep-fry chicken packages over low heat 1½ minutes. Remove and drain. Place packages on serving plate and serve. Unwrap before eating.

You may substitute beef tenderloin, fish filets or shrimp for the chicken and add Chinese sausage, ham, green peas, celery, onion or carrot slices as desired.

Oil may be reused for all these stir-fried dishes unless it burns or develops an off-taste. If necessary, strain it and add a little new oil to refresh it.

STIR-FRIED SHRIMP WITH GARLIC

⅔ pound medium size fresh shrimp
1 teaspoon ginger wine
1½ teaspoons cornstarch
6 cups oil for deep-frying
1 teaspoon salt
½ teaspoon flavor enhancer
2 tablespoons chopped garlic
1½ teaspoons chopped fresh hot red pepper

1. Rinse and cut antennae and all appendages from shrimp while still in shells. Devein by cutting through the shell. Mix with ginger wine and cornstarch and let sit 20 minutes.
2. Heat oil; deep-fry shrimp over high heat 1½ minutes. Remove and drain. Remove all oil from pan.
3. Return shrimp to pan with salt, flavor enhancer, garlic and red pepper and stir-fry until fragrant and ingredients are well mixed. Remove to serving plate and serve or keep warm while preparing remaining dishes.

This is a Peking-style dish. Leaving the shells on gives the shrimp a pleasing color. Use the three or four-inch long thin, fresh red peppers. Jalapeño may be substituted. Leaving the seeds and/or peppers in makes the dish hotter.

STIR-FRIED BEEF WITH OYSTER SAUCE

½ pound flank steak or beef tenderloin
Soy sauce
Rice wine
Water
Cornstarch
Oil
6 (1-inch) sections green onion
6 slices ginger root
1½ tablespoons oyster or soy sauce
¼ teaspoon flavor enhancer
¼ teaspoon sugar
¼ teaspoon black pepper
¼ teaspoon sesame oil

1. Remove any fat or tough membrane from beef. Cut across the grain into thin bite-size pieces. Mix with 1 tablespoon soy sauce, 1 teaspoon rice wine, 5 tablespoons water and 2 teaspoons cornstarch and let soak 1 hour. Mix with 1 tablespoon oil.
2. Heat 3 cups oil for deep-frying and deep-fry meat slices over medium heat 20 seconds or until changed in color. Remove and drain. Remove all but 2 tablespoons oil from pan and reheat. Stir-fry green onion and ginger until fragrant. Add beef slices, 1½ teaspoons rice wine, oyster sauce, flavor enhancer, sugar, pepper, ¼ teaspoon sesame oil, 1½ table-spoons water and 1 teaspoon cornstarch. Toss lightly to mix ingredients and remove to serving plate. Serve or keep warm while preparing remaining dishes.

STIR-FRIED CHICKEN WITH WALNUTS

¾ pound boneless chicken
1 tablespoon ginger wine
Salt
1 egg white
Cornstarch
4 cups water
2 cups walnut halves
Oil
6 (1-inch) sections green onion
6 slices ginger root
1 teaspoon rice wine
½ teaspoon sesame oil
½ teaspoon flavor enhancer
¼ teaspoon black pepper

1. Pound chicken flat; cut into bite-size pieces. Mix with ginger wine, 1 teaspoon salt and egg white and let sit 20 minutes. Add 1 tablespoon cornstarch and mix well.
2. Add water and 1 teaspoon salt to walnuts. Simmer over low heat 8 minutes; remove walnuts and drain on paper towels. When dry, rub off papery covering, then deep-fry in 3 cups oil over low heat 8 minutes until golden. Remove and drain.
3. Reheat pan and oil. Deep-fry chicken 30 seconds. When it changes color, remove.
4. Remove all but 2 tablespoons oil from the pan. Stir-fry green onion and ginger until fragrant. Add chicken, rice wine, 1 teaspoon salt, sesame oil, flavor enhancer, pepper and walnuts.
5. Stir-fry until ingredients are mixed. Serve or keep warm while other dishes are being prepared.

Green peas, bamboo shoots, carrots, green pepper, mushrooms, hot red peppers or cashews may be substituted for walnuts (no need to simmer as directed for walnuts).

Boiling the walnuts eliminates any bitter taste they might have and loosens the papery covering so it can be rubbed off easily.

STIR-FRIED VEGETARIAN DISH

Fried gluten balls and su-tsang (bean threads) are both made from wheat flour. They may be purchased canned in a Chinese grocery store and may be stored for a long period of time.

Oil
1½ ounces bean curd, cut in sticks
3 ribs Chinese celery cabbage, bok choy or broccoli
    (about ⅔ pound)
Water
20 fried gluten balls
6 (1-inch) sections green onion
6 slices ginger root
1 tablespoon rice wine
4 tablespoons soy sauce
1 teaspoon flavor enhancer
1 tablespoon sugar
¼ teaspoon black pepper
1 teaspoon sesame oil
1 tablespoon vinegar
½ cup canned bamboo shoots, sliced
¼ cup thinly sliced carrots, partially cooked
1 cup Chinese wood ears, cut in half (soak in water about
    10 minutes to soften)
¼ cup Chinese black mushrooms (soaked in water to soften)
1 (2-ounce) roll su-tsang (bean threads)
1 teaspoon cornstarch

1. Heat 3 cups oil for deep frying. Deep-fry bean curd sticks about 1 minute over medium heat until golden brown. Remove and drain.
2. Cut each piece of cabbage into 4 sections. Heat 5 cups water to boiling. Add cabbage and cook 2 minutes. Remove and drain and place in cold water until cool. Drain. Cook fried gluten balls and bean curd sticks in boiling water 3 minutes to remove excess oil. Remove and drain. Cut bean curd sticks in 1½-inch pieces.
3. Heat pan and 3 tablespoons oil. Stir-fry green onion and ginger root until fragrant. Add rice wine to 2 cups water, soy sauce, flavor enhancer, sugar, black pepper, sesame oil and vinegar.
4. Combine with cabbage, bamboo shoots, carrots, wood ears, mushrooms, su-tsang, fried gluten balls and bean curd stick sections. Cook over medium heat 5 minutes until liquid is almost gone.
5. Thicken with cornstarch which has been dissolved in 1 tablespoon water. Add 1 tablespoon oil. Toss lightly to mix all ingredients. Remove to serving plate and serve.

Chinese food is more interesting for groups of people than for one or two. When ordering in a restaurant, order one less dish than there are people in your party plus an appetizer, soup and boiled rice. The Chinese seldom eat elaborate desserts. They have fruit or simple sweets. If you would like to add a dessert to this menu, canned chilled lychee nuts would be appropriate.

Confederate House

Dinner for Six

Hickory Smoked Shrimp

Wilhelmina Salad

Beer Batter Fried Trout

Sautéed Mushrooms

Hush Puppies

Confederate Pie

Wine:
With Shrimp and Salad—Chalone Chardonnay
With Trout—Mark West Chardonnay
After Dinner—Quady Port Artist's Edition

Gordon Edge, Owner
Claude Wilson, Chef

The Confederate House has been an "in" restaurant with Houstonians for thirty-two years, but its formula for success—sophisticated Southern home cooking using only the freshest and best quality ingredients—is suddenly new again.

Founded and owned by Gordon Edge, the Confederate House was a fixture for years on San Felipe where it catered to established diners who fancied bourbon-and-branch water as an apéritif and well-done beef as an entrée. The restaurant moved a few blocks away to its present location in Highland Village seven years ago and added luncheon service at that time. In the past three years, the restaurant has earned a reputation for one of the most outstanding wine lists in the city. It is a knowledgeable mixture of the best French Burgundies and Bordeaux and an extensive collection of exceptional California wines.

"At lunch, we do more recipe-type cooking and dishes that appeal to the business people who come," says Bill Edge, son of the owner. Chef Claude Wilson draws on his Southern background to do such dishes as gumbo, roast pork with cornbread dressing and fried catfish as daily specials. Fudge pie, pecan balls with hot fudge sauce and Confederate Pie, a light textured lemon chess pie typical of the South, are always on the menu.

"At night, it's mainly simple, Southern-style cooking that shows off the quality of the ingredients, like our prime beef, frog legs, quail and fresh fish and seafood. Each item is simply prepared to bring out its best. We don't do elaborate sauces, but we concentrate on careful preparation." For its Chicken Fried Steak, the Confederate House even uses expensive beef rib eye. The steak is the most popular item on the menu day and night. Many of their customers from nearby River Oaks come in several evenings a week and celebrate family occasions there as well.

Ivory white paneling and columns, arched windows with velvet draperies and oil paintings of ancestors and Confederate generals add to the dining room's air of Southern gentility.

4007 Westheimer

HICKORY SMOKED SHRIMP

4 tablespoons butter, melted
3 tablespoons Worcestershire sauce
Juice of 1 lemon
42 shrimp (26-30 count), peeled and deveined, with tails left on
Parsley sprigs and lemon wedges for garnish

1. Mix melted butter, Worcestershire sauce and lemon juice.
2. Dab sauce on shrimp and arrange on broiler pan.
3. Broil 6 to 8 minutes, just until done.
4. Serve 7 on each plate garnished with a sprig of parsley and a
   lemon wedge.

*The combination of the butter, Worcestershire and lemon juice
gives the shrimp sauce its hickory-smoked flavor.*

WILHELMINA SALAD

2 large heads iceberg lettuce, washed and torn in pieces
2 medium heads romaine, broken up
2 large or 3 small endive, pulled apart
1½ bunches fresh watercress, chopped
2½ avocados, peeled and diced
2 tomatoes, diced
1 cup crumbled Roquefort
2 cups oil and vinegar dressing (about ½ cup vinegar, 1½ cups oil, mixed)

1. Combine iceberg lettuce, romaine, endive and watercress in
   salad bowl.
2. Add avocado, tomatoes and Roquefort.
3. Toss with just enough oil and vinegar to moisten.

*The salad should not be too wet with oil and vinegar. Adjust amount
needed according to amount of greens and your own taste, using two
parts oil to one part vinegar. Toss so that Roquefort is well dispersed
through salad.*

BEER BATTER FRIED TROUT

6 trout filets
1 cup all-purpose flour
2½ (12-ounce) cans beer
1 teaspoon cayenne pepper
Tartar Sauce

1. Mix flour, beer and cayenne in a blender until smooth and the consistency of a thick pancake batter. Refrigerate batter about 1 to 1½ hours.
2. Dip filets in batter and drop into hot, deep fat (350 degrees) and deep-fry.
3. Remove from fat with slotted spoon and drain on paper towels. Serve with **Tartar Sauce.**

Be sure batter is thick and well chilled. To tell if oil for deep frying is hot enough, shake a little flour in it. If it foams up, it is ready.

CONFEDERATE HOUSE TARTAR SAUCE

1 onion, finely chopped
⅓ cup dill pickle relish, well-drained
⅓ cup sweet pickle relish, well-drained
3 tablespoons horseradish
1½ teaspoons prepared mustard
Juice of ½ lemon
3 cups real mayonnaise
2 tablespoons ketchup

1. Combine chopped onion, well-drained pickle relishes, horseradish, mustard and lemon juice.
2. Add mayonnaise and ketchup, mixing well. Keep refrigerated.

Use a thick, heavy-style real mayonnaise for best results and taste.

SAUTEED MUSHROOMS

5 tablespoons butter
½ cup finely chopped onion
2 pounds button mushrooms, sliced in half
⅓ cup dry cocktail sherry

1. Melt butter in a large skillet. Add onion and sauté until tender
   but not brown.
2. Mix in mushrooms and cook 8 to 9 minutes, stirring often.
3. Just before serving, stir in sherry.

*Select small, firm button mushrooms so that when they are cut in
half they will be bite-size.*

HUSH PUPPIES

2 cups stone-ground corn meal
1 cup all-purpose flour
1 bunch green onions, finely chopped
1 medium onion, finely chopped
3 slices bacon, cooked crisp and chopped
Bacon drippings
1 egg
1 teaspoon cayenne pepper
Salt
2 teaspoons sugar
2 cups water (approximately)

1. Mix all ingredients in order, adding enough water to make a very thick, dry batter.
2. Roll in balls about the size of walnuts.
3. Fry in deep hot fat (350 degrees). Brown on both sides, flipping hush puppies if necessary. Drain on paper towels. Makes about 18, or 3 per serving.

Batter should be neither bone dry nor runny. Be sure fat is hot enough and stays hot while hush puppies are cooking.

CONFEDERATE PIE
(Lemon Chess Pie)

¼ pound butter, melted
6 eggs
2 cups sugar
⅓ cup cornstarch
½ cup half-and-half
Juice of 6 lemons
1 (9-inch) unbaked pie shell

1. Mix melted butter with eggs and sugar in electric mixer on
   medium speed 2 to 3 minutes, or until well mixed.
2. Stir cornstarch into half-and-half to dissolve, then pour into
   egg mixture.
3. Add lemon juice and stir until well mixed.
4. Pour into pie shell. Bake 1½ hours at 300 degrees until brown on
   top and done in center.

*To tell if pie is done, shake pan gently. Filling should shiver in the
middle and not be runny.*

D'Amico's
Italian Restaurant

Dinner for Four

Fritto di Mozzarella

Capellini Siciliana

Insalata di Arancia

Spiedini di Gamberi dell' Adriatico

Petti di Pollo Fiorentina

Chocolate Cheesecake

Caffè d'Amico

Wine:
With Fritto and Capellini—Spanna Dessilani 1971
With Shrimp and Chicken—Frascati Fontana Candida
1978

Damian Mandola, Charles Petronella and
Anthony Rao, Owners
Anthony Rao, Chef

D'Amico's is a young Houston version of the friendly Italian trattoria. The three cousins who are owners—Damian Mandola, Charles Petronella and Anthony Rao—bring to the restaurant a background of loving Italian home cooking and la dolce vita. The forerunner of the restaurant, Damian's Fine Italian Foods, opened in 1975 in Huntsville, Texas. D'Amico's (named for a fourth original partner) was the culmination of a dream to own a restaurant in Houston.

Since D'Amico's opened in December, 1977 it has evolved into a polished purveyor of veal, seafood and pasta dishes of southern Italian origin with northern Italian flair. There is a new menu and the pasta is now made in-house. Among the out-of-the-ordinary dishes are a salad of fresh tomato and mozzarella cheese chunks tossed in olive oil and herbs, Trout Toto (a filet of trout with fresh crab), Cuscinetti (veal pillows stuffed with ham and Mozzarella, dipped in egg, then sautéed in a sauce touched with Marsala) and a delectable dessert from the handsome tiered dessert cart, Oranges Grand Marnier.

Tableside preparation of zabaglione is a treat, especially when the waiter curls the wrapper from the amaretto cookie used as a garnish and flames it for you to make a wish. If it ascends, your wish will come true—so the story goes. For special occasions, expect a serenade in Italian from the uniformed waiters.

The atmosphere is relaxed and casual. Rose-hued walls set the color scheme. Pale pink linens, fringed parasol lamps, lace curtains, antiques, hanging plants and framed family portraits combine in an appealing front-parlor decor. Sometimes there's a strolling accordionist. "D'Amico means 'in the house of a friend', and we want our customers to feel that they have come to our house. A lot of restaurants lose their friend-liness and become very cold when they become successful. We hope to achieve success and good service, but also to keep that touch of personal friendliness because Italians are amiable people. We like to have a good time, and we like our customers to have a good time," says Damian Mandola.

2407 Westheimer

FRITTO DI MOZZARELLA

8 slices mozzarella cheese, cut ¼-inch thick
4 eggs, beaten
2 cups dry bread crumbs
Vegetable oil for deep frying
Sauce Marinara

Dip each cheese slice in egg, then in breadcrumbs; repeat a second time. Deep-fry in oil until golden brown. Prepare in advance and refrigerate, then fry when ready to serve, if desired. Serve with Sauce Marinara.

Sauce Marinara

2 cloves garlic
¼ cup olive oil
2 cups canned whole tomatoes with juice
1 teaspoon sugar
Pinch of oregano
Salt and pepper to taste

1. Sauté the garlic in the olive oil over low heat until the garlic starts to take on a brown color.
2. Add the tomatoes by hand-crushing into the pan.
3. Add sugar, oregano, salt and pepper to taste. Simmer 10 minutes.

This is a good dish to prepare ahead of time. It's much more successful if the cheese is well chilled before deep-frying. The oil should be the proper temperature so the dish is not greasy. The sauce is versatile and can be served with other dishes.

CAPELLINI SICILIANA

1 small eggplant, peeled
Salt
¼ cup olive oil
2 tablespoons chopped onion
2 cloves garlic, chopped
2 cups canned whole tomatoes with juice
4 leaves fresh basil or a pinch of dried basil
½ pound capellini pasta
½ cup ricotta cheese
1 tablespoon capers
Pepper
¼ cup freshly grated Parmesan cheese

1. Bring 4 quarts salted water to a boil.
2. Remove ends from eggplant and cut in 2-inch cubes. Salt the eggplant and set in a colander for 30 minutes to drain off the bitter juices. After 30 minutes, wash salt off eggplant and squeeze dry in a towel.
3. Heat olive oil in a medium-size frying pan. Brown the eggplant in oil. When brown, remove with a slotted spoon. Reduce heat to low and add onions and garlic and sauté 5 minutes.
4. Crush tomatoes and add to the frying pan with their juice.
5. Return the eggplant to pan and add basil, salt and pepper to taste. Simmer 10 minutes.
6. Drop the capellini in boiling salted water and cook until done but still firm (al dente).
7. Quickly toss pasta, ricotta, capers, Parmesan and tomato-eggplant sauce together in a bowl. Remove to a platter and serve immediately.

INSALATA DI ARANCIA
(Orange Salad)

1 cucumber
1 large orange
5 or 6 small red radishes
A few fresh mint leaves
Salt
Olive oil
Freshly squeezed juice of ½ lemon

1. If the skin of the cucumber is waxed, peel it. If not, scrub it under cold running water. Wipe dry. Cut in the thinnest possible rounds. Place them in a salad bowl.
2. Peel the orange, taking care to remove all the white pith. Cut the orange into thin, round slices. Cut these in half, or if orange is very large, in four sections. Pick out all the seeds. Put orange in bowl.
3. Rinse and scrub the radishes, but do not peel. Cut in very thin rounds. Add to the bowl.
4. Tear mint leaves in small pieces and add them to the salad bowl.
5. Dress with salt, olive oil and lemon juice. Toss thoroughly and serve at once.

This is based on an old Italian dish that my grandfather and father used to make, says Damian Mandola. "My grandfather used only oranges with a little olive oil."

SPIEDINI DI GAMBERI DELL' ADREATICO
(Skewered Shrimp Char-broiled Adriatic Fashion)

1½ pounds small shrimp
3½ tablespoons olive oil
3½ tablespoons vegetable oil
⅔ cup fine, dry unflavored bread crumbs
½ teaspoon very finely chopped garlic
2 teaspoons finely chopped fresh parsley
¾ teaspoon salt
5 or 6 twists of the pepper mill of freshly ground pepper
Lemon wedges

1. Preheat broiler to its maximum setting. The broiler must be heated at least 15 minutes before the shrimp is to be cooked.
2. Shell and devein shrimp. Wash in cold water and pat thoroughly dry with a paper towel.
3. Put shrimp in large mixing bowl. Add as much of the two oils (mix in equal parts) and of the bread crumbs as you need to obtain an even, light, creamy coating on all the shrimp. When they are well coated, add chopped garlic, parsley, salt and pepper and mix well. Let shrimp steep in the marinade at least 20 minutes at room temperature.
4. Have ready some flat, double-edged skewers. Skewer the shrimp lengthwise, 5 or more shrimp per skewer, depending on the size. As you skewer each shrimp, curl and bend one end inward so that the skewer goes through the shrimp at three points. This is to make sure that the shrimp won't slip as you turn the skewer.
5. Cook shrimp in broiler no more than 3 minutes on one side and 2 minutes on the other, even less if the shrimp is very small. Each side is done as soon as a crisp golden crust forms.
6. Serve piping hot on the skewers with lemon wedges on the side.

Add only as much of the two oils and bread crumbs as necessary. Do not add all at once because you may not need it all. However, if you are working with very tiny shrimp, you may need even more. In any case, always use one part olive oil to one part vegetable oil.

PETTI DI POLLO FIORENTINA
(Chicken Breast Florentine)

1 (10-ounce) package fresh spinach
4 quarts boiling salted water
1 cup vegetable oil
4 chicken breast halves, boned
Flour
4 eggs, beaten
2 tablespoons butter
Salt and pepper
White Sauce
½ cup freshly grated Parmesan cheese

1. Remove stems from spinach and wash in two or three changes of water. Drop spinach in boiling salted water, cook and drain well in a colander.
2. Heat oil in a skillet. Dredge chicken breasts in flour and dip in egg. Sauté in oil, browning on both sides.
3. Melt butter in a sauté pan. Add spinach and sauté 3 minutes; season with salt and pepper. Place spinach on an ovenproof serving platter and arrange chicken over it. Top with **White Sauce** and sprinkle with grated Parmesan. Place the platter under broiler 2 to 3 minutes or until cheese is browned.

White Sauce

2 cups milk
4 tablespoons butter
3 tablespoons flour
¼ teaspoon salt
Pinch of nutmeg

1. Heat milk in a saucepan until bubbles form at edges (scald).
2. Melt butter over low heat in a heavy 4 to 6-cup saucepan.
3. When butter is melted, add the flour, stirring constantly with a wooden spoon or wire whisk. Let flour and butter cook 2 minutes, stirring constantly. Do not let the flour brown or take on a color.
4. Off the heat, add the hot milk, 2 tablespoons at a time, stirring constantly, until about ½ cup milk has been added. Then you can add ¼ cup at a time, still stirring constantly with a wooden spoon or whisk.
5. When all the milk has been incorporated, turn heat to low and add the salt and nutmeg. Cook, stirring, until sauce is thickened and smooth.

The sauce and the spinach may be made ahead of time and reheated when you are ready to fry the chicken. However, do not fry chicken until you are ready to serve.

D'AMICO'S CHOCOLATE CHEESECAKE

Crust

2 cups graham cracker crumbs
1 cup sugar
½ pound butter, melted

Thoroughly mix crumbs, sugar and butter and press into a 9-inch spring-form pan.

Filling

3 eggs
1 pound cream cheese, softened
1 cup sugar
1 teaspoon vanilla extract
1 teaspoon almond extract, or more to taste
1 pound sour cream
¼ cup chocolate extract

1. Preheat oven to 350 degrees. Beat eggs in a large bowl.
2. Add cream cheese and blend until smooth.
3. Pour sugar into the mixture, forming a pile. Top sugar pile with vanilla and almond extracts and blend until smooth with mixer.
4. Add sour cream and blend thoroughly.
5. Fill crust three-fourths full.
6. To the remaining mixture, add chocolate extract and blend well. Pour the chocolate mixture over the first, filling the pie crust.
7. Bake in preheated oven 40 to 45 minutes or until cake is set. Remove from oven.
8. Chill in the refrigerator at least 2 hours, or until firm.

This is an extremely popular dessert at D'Amico's. Many people refer to it as the Amaretto Cheesecake because of the pronounced almond flavoring, but it has no amaretto in it. The chocolate extract may be difficult to find. Check fine food shops or stores that carry a complete line of flavorings. McCormick's is one brand.

CAFFE D'AMICO

Per serving:

1 ounce amaretto
¼ ounce Aurum
Hot coffee
Whipped cream
Dash of nutmeg
1 maraschino cherry with stem

1. Mix liqueurs and coffee in glass desired.
2. Top with a flourish of whipped cream to the rim of the glass.
3. Sprinkle with nutmeg and garnish with cherry. Serve while coffee is hot.

Aurum is an Italian orange-flavored liqueur.

Foulard's
Restaurant

Dinner for Four

Shrimp Foulard's

Chilled Cream of Avocado

Poached Filet of Salmon, Clarice

Strawberry Sorbet

Pheasant Sautéed, Foulard

Sautéed Asparagus

Pomme Macaire

Crêpes, Del Carmen

Wine:

With Shrimp—Muscadet Marquis de Goulaine 1978
With Salmon—Château Oliver Grand Cru Classé 1976
With Pheasant—Chambolle-Musigny 1969
With Crêpes—Sauternes Château Voigny 1971

Edmond M. Foulard, Owner and Chef
Paul Plouff, Executive Chef
Frances Keogh, Manager
Martin A. Robert, Maître d'

Foulard's provides classic French food in the setting of a provincial inn. Rough white stone exteriors are offset with heavy beams and a water wheel at the entrance. Appealingly elegant interiors are a mix of coral and soft green florals, coral wainscoting, antiques and paintings. They are a foil for the mural in the main dining room done by Houston artist Nione Carlson as a theme-setter for the restaurant.

Chef-owner Edmond M. Foulard commands respect as a chef par excellence and a peerless sauce and soup cook. For Chef Foulard and his wife Annemarie, the award-winning restaurant is the culmination of a dream. Canadian-born of French parents, Foulard early set his sights on America. He says his greatest honor was becoming an American citizen in 1955.

He apprenticed at age thirteen in Nantes, France, then worked for Prunier's in Paris. Later he acquired his own restaurant in Paris, then a second and third. He came to the United States after World War II and moved to Houston in 1962. The Foulards opened their own restaurant in 1966. It was moved to another location in 1971, then to the present site, which Foulard personally designed, in 1976.

Countless Houstonians have learned to appreciate fine food and have developed culinary expertise at the Chef's cooking school at the restaurant. He is a member of the American Academy of Chefs and the Chevalier de la Confrerie de la Chaine des Rotisseurs. He holds the Golden Toque award from the American Institute of Chefs.

The restaurant has received several commendations, including the *Holiday* Award since 1977. "The restaurant and cooking are my life," Foulard says. "After 55 years, I still love to cook."

1001 Westheimer in Carillon Center

SHRIMP FOULARD'S

20 medium-large shrimp
Flour
Clarified butter
1 clove garlic, finely ground
4 tablespoons crab meat
¼ cup dry white wine
1 cup whipping cream
Salt and white pepper
Grated nutmeg
Chopped fresh parsley

1. Peel and devein shrimp. Dredge in flour and shake off excess.
2. Sauté shrimp in hot clarified butter. When nicely colored, discard the
   frying butter and add the garlic, crab and wine to the pan.
3. Cover with a lid for 1 or 2 minutes or until liquid has evaporated.
   Stir in whipping cream.
4. Season with salt, white pepper and a dash of nutmeg. Garnish with
   chopped parsley.
5. Serve shrimp in individual casseroles or four small ramekins.

*To clarify butter, melt butter in a deep saucepan over low heat.
Continue heating until foam disappears from top and there is sediment
in bottom of pan. When perfectly clear, remove from heat and skim
any brown crust from top. Pour off the clear butter and discard
sediment. Clarified butter doesn't burn as easily as whole butter and
it adds richness.*

CHILLED CREAM OF AVOCADO

1 large avocado
1½ cups light chicken broth
Juice of ¼ lime
Salt and white pepper
1 cup whipping cream
1 teaspoon red caviar

1. Peel avocado and remove pit.
2. Blend avocado with broth in a blender; bring to a boil and boil the
   mixture for a second, stirring lightly.
3. Add lime juice, salt and pepper to taste. Let cool.
4. Add cream; mix well.
5. Gently fold in caviar.
6. Serve in small soup cups.

POACHED FILET OF SALMON, CLARICE

4 (6-ounce) salmon filets
Court bouillon
2 medium shallots, finely chopped
2 medium mushrooms, finely chopped
½ cup fish velouté
¼ cup precooked, finely chopped spinach
½ cup **Hollandaise**
½ cup whipped cream
Salt and white pepper
Grated nutmeg

1. Poach the salmon in court bouillon a few minutes, until tender.
2. In another saucepan, combine the shallots and mushrooms with a little of the bouillon. Bring to a fast boil and cook until liquid is reduced.
3. Lightly fold in velouté, spinach, Hollandaise and whipped cream. Season to taste with salt, pepper and nutmeg.
4. Arrange the poached salmon on a serving platter. Wipe it dry and cover with the sauce. Glaze under a broiler or a salamander and serve at once.

Court bouillon is a poaching liquid. Make with half a carrot, one small onion and half a celery rib, thinly sliced; 3 or 4 parsley stems, 3 or 4 peppercorns, a small bay leaf, salt, fish bones and water or a combination of water and dry white wine in equal proportions to cover fish. Strain and cool before using.

A velouté is the same as a bechamel (cream sauce) except it is made with stock instead of milk. The velouté takes the name of whatever stock it is made with, such as fish or chicken.

Hollandaise

3 egg yolks
2 tablespoons water
1½ teaspoons lemon juice
⅛ teaspoon salt
Pinch of white pepper
1 cup warm clarified butter

1. Combine egg yolks, water, lemon juice, salt and pepper and beat until smooth and creamy. Turn into a double boiler and whip continuously until the egg yolks thicken. Remove from heat.
2. Gradually pour in the warm butter, beating to incorporate it into the sauce.
3. Correct seasoning to your taste and keep warm.

A Hollandaise should always be served within the hour in which it has been made.

STRAWBERRY SORBET

1 cup sweet sauterne
Grated rind and juice of 1 lemon
Juice of ½ orange
½ cup water
1 cup sugar
2 cups puréed strawberries
2 ounces strawberry liqueur
2 ounces Kirsch (clear cherry brandy)

1. Mix the sauterne, lemon and orange juices, lemon rind, water, sugar and strawberries in a saucepan and bring to a boil.
2. Let simmer exactly 5 minutes.
3. Let the mixture cool.
4. Stir in both liqueurs and freeze.

This serves as a palate refresher between courses, but could be used on another occasion as a light dessert.

PHEASANT SAUTEED, FOULARD

2 pheasants, partly boned and disjointed
Salt and white pepper
Flour
Clarified butter
8 breakfast link sausages
24 small, whole, fresh mushrooms
½ tablespoon chopped shallots
¼ cup brandy
½ cup brown sauce
¼ cup whipping cream
4 tablespoons fresh butter
4 precooked artichoke bottoms
6 tablespoons precooked spinach
Grated cheese of your choice

1. Cut pheasants in six pieces each, discarding wings and carcasses or saving for another use. You should have two legs, two thighs and two breast halves per bird.
2. Preheat oven to 375 degrees.
3. Season pheasant meat with salt and pepper, dredge in flour and sauté in ovenproof sauté pan in a little hot clarified butter until golden blond on all sides.
4. Discard the frying fat and place pheasant in preheated oven until done, about 15 to 20 minutes depending on size. When half done, add sausages and mushrooms to the pan.
5. When done, add shallots. Transfer pan to top of range.
6. Add brandy and ignite. Let flame burn out.
7. Finish on top of the range by stirring in the brown sauce, cream and fresh butter. Correct the seasoning with salt and pepper.
8. Serve with a hot artichoke bottom filled with chopped spinach and topped with grated cheese.

Good cooking means simple, clean cooking. By clean, I mean no heavy frying in fat, even clarified butter or oil. Instead, lightly sauté, pour off all cooking fat, then finish the dish in the oven by adding a little fresh butter. Don't allow it to get so hot it fries or burns. The fresh butter smooths the sauce and helps digestion, I think.

SAUTEED ASPARAGUS

1 to 1½ pounds fresh asparagus (white or green)
Butter
Few drops of dry white wine

1. Wash asparagus; peel and trim stalks to the same size. Tie in a bundle.
2. Cook in boiling salted water in a deep pan or steamer pan with a rack until tender-crisp.
3. Arrange asparagus spears flat in an ovenproof sauté pan and sauté in a little butter and a few drops of white wine in a 400-degree oven until tender.

POMME MACAIRE

1 pound boiling potatoes
Salt and white pepper
Grated nutmeg
1 egg yolk
¼ cup whipping cream
2 tablespoons fresh butter
Clarified butter

1. Peel potatoes and boil in salted water. Drain well and dry them a little in a low oven. (Or, bake the potatoes and scoop out the pulp.)
2. Mash potatoes and season with salt, pepper and nutmeg.
3. Add egg yolk, cream and fresh butter. Taste and correct the seasoning if necessary.
4. When almost ready to serve, cover bottom of an ovenproof frying pan with clarified butter and fill it with the potato mixture.
5. Bake in a 425-degree oven until hot and golden brown.
6. Turn the potatoes out on a plate and cut in wedges to serve.

CRÊPES, DEL CARMEN

1 tablespoon butter
Grated rind of 1 lemon
Grated rind of 1 orange
2 teaspoons lemon juice
4 tablespoons orange juice
8 Crêpes
4 ounces brandy
4 ounces Triple Sec
4 ounces Galliano liqueur

1. Melt butter in a chafing dish with lemon and orange rind.
2. Add lemon and orange juice and simmer until mixture forms a light syrup.
3. Add the crêpes and turn them over in the liquid. When they are hot, add the brandy and liqueurs and ignite.
4. Serve.

Crêpes

¼ cup flour
½ cup eggs (about 3 medium eggs)
2 tablespoons oil
½ cup half-and-half
Pinch of salt

1. Combine flour, eggs, oil, half-and-half and salt; beat. Strain through a fine strainer.
2. Heat a non-stick pan, 5 or 6 inches in diameter, until moderately hot.
3. Cover the bottom of the pan with a very thin coating of the batter, using about ¾ of an ounce. Let it barely brown and set for a few seconds, then flip the crêpe over to cook evenly on the other side.
4. Continue in same manner until all batter has been used.

The Good Eats Cafe

Dinner for Six

Pedernales Fruit Shake

Savannah-Style Beer-Batter Fried Chicken

Sawmill Gravy

Country Squash Casserole

Fresh Okra and Tomatoes

Southern Style Jalapeño Corn Bread Muffins

Peanut Butter Pie

Beverage:
Beer, Light Beer or Iced Tea

Toni, Spero and Ernie Criezis, Owner's

The Good Eats Cafe is a comfortable multi-level structure which is an instant jaunt down memory lane to the cafes of the '30s and '40s. The barnlike building seats 350 and is chock-to-the-rafters with plants, plaques, old signs and a veritable museum of Texan and Southern antiques.

The winning philosophy behind this latest venture of the Criezis family (who have already given Houston the Bowery, Fat Ernie's, Harlow's and the Great Caruso) is fresh, home-cooked foods prepared daily by a platoon of small-town-style Texas cooks. Although a newcomer to the scene (it opened in April, 1980) it is quickly attaining star status as a trendsetter.

Waitresses wearing cafe whites and huge shoulder flowers of the period serve up bountiful portions of a hit parade of Texas specials such as jalapeno corn bread. The menu also rotates blueplate specials such as Chicken and Dumplings, Baked Chicken and Dressing, Pot Roast and Son-of-a-Gun Stew. From time to time it features old-fashioned meatloaf, barbecue and vegetable plates. Buckets of salad and homemade soup are served with all dinner specials. The menu of the day is usually the same for the lunchtime blueplates and at dinner for completely family-style meals. Big, beefy burgers, fried shrimp and fries are other options. Downhome desserts include fruit cobblers, bread pudding and homemade pie.

The music, recorded and live (Sundays only), also is a charming throwback to the thirties and forties—old cowboy melodies, West Texas polkas, Cajun tunes and Mexican border cantina music. Everyone from the after-church crowd on Sundays to blue-collar types and visiting celebrities, and recently a French baron and baroness and the Crown Prince of Denmark, keep the place jammed to capacity at almost any hours.

2305 S. Voss Road

PEDERNALES FRUIT SHAKE

1 cup sliced fresh strawberries
1 banana, sliced
1 cup chopped pitted dates
10 ounces vanilla ice cream
Nutmeg

1. Combine strawberries, banana, dates and ice cream in blender container and blend well.
2. Pour into stemmed glasses, sprinkle with nutmeg and serve. Makes 2.

SAVANNAH-STYLE BEER-BATTER FRIED CHICKEN

2 eggs, slightly beaten
⅔ cup beer
1 cup all-purpose flour
½ teaspoon salt
2 tablespoons melted shortening or oil
2 (2 to 3-pound) broiler-fryers, cut up
Oil for deep-frying

1. Combine slightly beaten eggs with beer. Slowly beat in flour, salt and oil until the batter is smooth.
2. Dip chicken pieces into batter and drain.
3. Drop into heated oil (375 degrees). Deep-fry 15 to 20 minutes until golden brown. As pieces get done, keep warm in the oven preheated to its lowest setting. Drain on paper towels.

Be sure chicken pieces are dry before dipping them in the batter and deep-fry only a few pieces at a time so oil remains at a constant temperature. Some Southern cooks like to soak chicken in milk or buttermilk an hour before frying in a plain batter.

There are two styles of Southern fried chicken: it may be fried crisp and served with cream gravy on the side or fried in a covered pan until brown on one side, turned and cooked until done, then steamed in the gravy.

Sawmill Gravy

¼ cup bacon grease
¾ cup all-purpose flour
3 cups milk, heated
1½ teaspoons freshly ground black pepper
Salt to taste

1. Heat bacon fat until hot in skillet, then mix in flour.
2. Pour in heated milk gradually, stirring constantly. Whisk until slightly thickened and smooth.
3. While gravy simmers, add pepper and salt. Simmer until thick. This makes about 1 quart.

COUNTRY SQUASH CASSEROLE

2 pounds yellow squash, cut up
½ to 1 cup sour cream
1 (10¾-ounce) can condensed cream of chicken soup
1 small onion, chopped
Salt and pepper to taste
1 carrot, grated
Herb-seasoned bread crumbs
Butter

1. Cut squash in chunks and drop into boiling water. Cook covered until soft. Drain well and mash. You should have about 4 cups.
2. Combine squash in bowl with sour cream, undiluted soup, onion, salt, pepper and grated carrot.
3. Sprinkle an even layer of herb-seasoned bread crumbs on the bottom of a shallow 2-quart casserole. Add squash mixture and cover with another layer of crumbs. Dot generously with butter.
4. Bake at 350 degrees 30 to 40 minutes.

Drain squash well or mixture may be watery. Add sour cream as desired for consistency and richness. If using glass baking dish, reduce oven temperature by twenty-five degrees.

FRESH OKRA AND TOMATOES

3 to 4 pieces bacon, cut up
1½ cups water
1 onion, chopped
1 pound fresh okra, trimmed and cut in ½-inch pieces
1(1-pound) can peeled whole tomatoes
Salt and pepper to taste

1. Sauté bacon until crisp.
2. Combine bacon with water in 3-quart saucepan and heat until almost boiling. Add onion, okra, tomatoes and salt and pepper to taste. Simmer covered about 15 to 20 minutes.

Okra, originally called gombo with an "o", is used in Cajun cooking to thicken and flavor gumbo and stews. Some people object to it because they think it is slimy, but sliminess can be avoided if you don't cut into the seed pods when you are trimming the top and don't overcook. To preserve the color, never cook in iron, copper or tin pans. Use stainless steel, porcelainized enamel or glass.

SOUTHERN STYLE JALAPEÑO CORN BREAD MUFFINS

1 cup yellow corn meal
1 cup all-purpose flour
¼ cup sugar
4 teaspoons baking powder
½ teaspoon salt
1 cup milk
1 egg
¼ cup shortening or bacon drippings
½ cup cream-style corn
½ to 1 jalapeño pepper, chopped
½ teaspoon diced pimiento

1. Preheat oven to 350 degrees.
2. Combine corn meal, flour, sugar, baking powder and salt.
3. Add milk, egg, melted shortening and corn. Mix.
4. Stir in pepper and diced pimiento.
5. Pour into greased muffin pans and bake about 20 to 30 minutes.

PEANUT BUTTER PIE

3 eggs
½ cup dark corn syrup
½ cup creamy peanut butter
2 cups sugar
½ cup butter
2 cups chopped nuts (unsalted peanuts are good)
Pastry for a 9-inch pie crust

1. Preheat oven to 350 degrees.
2. Beat eggs and mix in all ingredients except nuts.
3. Pour into pie shell. Top with nuts and bake 30 minutes or until firm.

Dinner for Six

Oyster Velouté

Boston Butter Lettuce Salad

Veal Citron

Savarin

Flaming Café Amaretto

Wine:
With Soup—Trimbach Riesling
With Veal—Château Haut Corbin St.-Emilion
With Dessert—Taittinger Brut Champagne

Bob Williamson, General Manager, Hyatt Regency
Edward McClure, Food and Beverage Director
Peter Lehr, Executive Chef

Hugo's Window Box is the Hyatt Regency Hotel's showpiece restaurant. It appeals to those who take fine food seriously, such as well-traveled executives with offices downtown, and members of wine and food societies.

A glass box perched above the atrium lobby of the Hyatt, the Window Box is an oasis of emerald green and gold. It is festooned with myriad strings of tiny twinkle lights showering from the ceiling. Music by harpist Virginia Robbins is a relaxing mood-setter.

The hotel management has changed, but not the philosophy of providing award-winning food prepared by European-trained chefs. Hugo's has received the *Holiday* Award, Mobil Four-Star Award and the Epicurean Award since 1978. The food and beverage director and executive chef were recently installed in the prestigious gourmet society, the Confrerie de la Chaine des Rotisseurs.

Hugo's is known for its subtle touches like personalized matches, butter molded with the Hyatt crest and hot damp napkins provided at the end of the meal. Everyone is served appetizers which rotate seasonally between raw Belgian endive in a brandy snifter with a tangy sauce and mousse of gooseliver pâté on an artichoke bottom with French bread. Emphasis is on the freshest foodstuffs, many of which are flown in or purchased from special suppliers.

One of the most unique features is Hugo's 24, a culinary society of twenty-four elite Houston businessmen who regularly dine at the restaurant. They have special privileges including their own wine cabinets with gold keys.

1200 Louisiana

OYSTER VELOUTE

2 pounds fish heads, tails and bones
1 small onion, quartered
1 carrot, cut in chunks
2 ribs celery, chopped
Salt and pepper
1 bay leaf
2 to 3 cloves
24 oysters with their liquor
Beurre Manié

1. Place fish heads, tails and bones in a large pot and cover with
   2 quarts of cold water. Add onion, carrot, celery, salt, pepper,
   bay leaf and cloves. Bring to a boil and let simmer 2 to 3 hours
   or until reduced to 1 quart. Strain.
2. Add the oyster liquor to the stock. Over low heat, add **Beurre
   Manié** a little at a time and whisk until thoroughly blended. The
   sauce should simmer just a few minutes to eliminate the floury
   taste and thicken properly, but should not be allowed to boil.
3. Poach oysters in simmering salted water for 2 minute or until
   oysters float to the top and are ruffled. Add to velouté. Serve in
   soup bowls, allowing 4 oysters per serving.

Beurre Manié

4 tablespoons butter
8 tablespoons flour

Knead butter and flour together thoroughly. Roll into small balls.

BOSTON BUTTER LETTUCE SALAD

2 to 3 heads Boston leaf lettuce
1¼ to 1½ cups olive oil
½ cup tarragon vinegar
½ ounce fresh lemon juice
2 tablespoons finely chopped shallots
2 egg yolks
Salt and pepper

1. Trim, clean and wash lettuce. Pat dry.
2. Combine oil, vinegar, lemon juice and shallots. Whisk in egg yolks, salt and pepper.
3. Toss with lettuce.

Lettuce should be washed several times to remove all grit and sand.

VEAL CITRON

12 (3½-ounce) medallions of veal
Flour, salt and pepper
Butter
¼ cup fresh lemon juice
1 pint whipping cream
¼ cup demi-glace or brown sauce mix

1. Flour, salt and pepper each medallion lightly. Sauté quickly in butter and remove from pan. Keep warm.
2. Add lemon juice to hot pan and reduce, about 1 minute. Whisk in cream when lemon juice is concentrated.
3. Add demi-glace (or brown sauce) for color and flavor. Simmer until concentrated, but do not let sauce boil.
4. Serve over veal medallions.

The secret to a smooth sauce is letting the lemon juice concentrate itself for about a minute in the pan before you pour in the cold cream, then whisking it briskly over heat. If you don't let the lemon juice concentrate, the cream may break down when it is added.

Butter should be sizzling hot when veal is added.

SAVARIN

1 small package active dry yeast ($\frac{1}{3}$ ounce)
¼ cup lukewarm water (110 degrees)
1 tablespoon sugar
1½ cups sifted all-purpose flour
½ teaspoon salt
3 small eggs, beaten
¼ cup milk, warmed
⅔ cup butter, at room temperature

To serve:
6 scoops French vanilla ice cream
¾ cup chocolate fudge sauce, warmed
¼ to ½ cup sliced toasted almonds
1 ounce Swiss milk chocolate

1. Make starter dough: dissolve yeast in warm water with 1 teaspoon sugar and ½ cup flour. Let rise until doubled.
2. Combine remaining dough ingredients with the starter and let rise again until doubled. Punch down. Divide dough into ten rounds and place in savarin (small ring) molds. Let rise again until doubled.
3. Bake at 375 degrees for 25 to 30 minutes.
4. Place each cake in a 6 or 8-ounce stemmed glass. Top with a scoop of ice cream.
5. Cover with chocolate sauce, almonds and whipped cream.
6. Grate chocolate over the cream.

FLAMING CAFE AMARETTO

Lemon juice and sugar
¾ cup Amaretto liqueur
4 cups freshly brewed coffee
½ cup Galliano liqueur
½ cup unsweetened whipped cream
Zest of 1 lime

1. Using 6 to 8-ounce stemmed glasses, dip the rim of each glass in lemon juice, then in sugar.
2. Pour 1 ounce Amaretto into each glass and warm the liqueur over an open flame. When warm, light by tipping the glass carefully toward the flame until the liqueur is nearly spilling out.
3. Pour in the coffee and Galliano.
4. Top with unsweetened whipped cream.
5. Grate only the zest (the outermost skin) of the lime on top of the whipped cream. Place glass on plate and garnish with an Italian amaretti cookie.

La Quiche

The Continental Cafe

Dinner for Six

Strawberry Daiquiris

Liver Pâté

Liptauer Cheese

Seafood Gumbo

Cheddar Cheese Bread

Spinach Salad

Chicken Marsala

Carrot Cake

Wine:
Hugel or Dopff & Irion Gewürztraminer

Rudi Lechner, Owner

La Quiche began as a casual restaurant with sidewalk café atmosphere and quiche as the main menu item, but it is emerging as a full-fledged Continental restaurant with the theatrics of tableside cooking. "I like to cater to people's moods and I like guests to have a fun dining experience," says owner Rudi Lechner. "What I am trying to accomplish is an informal brasserie-café-gasthaus type of European restaurant where you can drop in anytime you like. I want people to feel comfortable whether they come in for a piece of quiche, drinks, a cup of coffee and a piece of strudel or a special-occasion meal."

The menu continues to reflect Lechner's solid background as a classically-trained chef. He apprenticed in a pastry shop in Austria and worked for the largest hotel chain in Europe before coming to the States. After stints as chef and food and beverage director for the Hyatt Regency, he decided to open his own quiche restaurant.

"Quiche is not a fancy item; in Europe it's a peasant food. It's also very versatile and nutritious," he says. Quiche remains one focal point on the menu, but people are increasingly attracted by the salad bar extra-ordinaire and homemade breads, Sunday brunch, an intriguing variety of Continental coffees and Very Special Cuisine items which are available after 6 p.m. A wine room with fireside library ambiance attracts many small luncheon, dinner and party groups.

2501 S. Gessner

STRAWBERRY DAIQUIRI

15 ripe strawberries
Sugar
6 ounces light rum
2 ounces lime juice
Ice cubes

1. Choose nice size strawberries, sprinkle with sugar and let them marinate several hours, about half a day. Drain.
2. In blender, combine berries, rum, lime juice and a few ice cubes. Blend until smooth. Serve in champagne glasses and garnish with a fresh strawberry.

LIVER PATE

4 ounces chicken fat
¼ cup chopped celery
¼ cup finely chopped onion
1 pound chicken livers
1 teaspoon thyme
1 teaspoon rosemary
1 teaspoon basil
1 teaspoon oregano
1 tablespoon Worcestershire sauce
1 tablespoon Cognac

1. Place chicken fat in skillet and cook (render) over medium heat until it is liquified. Remove any particles that do not dissolve.
2. Add celery and onion and sauté until vegetables are a light golden brown.
3. Add chicken livers, herbs and Worcestershire sauce. Simmer over low heat about 45 minutes.
4. Adding Cognac, run livers through a food mill or food processor to form a smooth paste. Chill.

Liver Pâté is a regular item on La Quiche's salad bar. It is excellent as an appetizer or snack with bagels or warm French bread.

LIPTAUER CHEESE

Liptauer cheese is one of the most popular and unique items on the salad bar at La Quiche.

¼ pound butter or margarine
¾ pound cream cheese, softened
¼ pound cottage cheese
2 tablespoons chopped fresh parsley
¼ cup finely diced red onion
1½ tablespoons paprika
1 tablespoon Colman's mustard
3 tablespoons Worcestershire sauce
1 tablespoon caraway seed

1. Beat the butter until very smooth and creamy with a rotary beater or electric blender.
2. Add cream cheese and beat until well blended and smooth.
3. Add cottage cheese, parsley, onion, paprika, dry mustard, Worcestershire sauce and caraway seed; whip until thoroughly blended.
4. Chill. Serve in crocks.

Liptauer is of Austrian origin. It is at its best when served with warm fresh French bread as an hors d'oeuvre, or a snack any time of day.

SEAFOOD GUMBO

Gumbo should reflect the taste of the cook. Experiment with the seasonings to develop a taste that is exciting to you. Chicken seasoned stock base and fish base are available where bouillon is sold in fine food shops and gourmet departments. The fish base enhances the flavor, but may be omitted if not available. Gumbo file, made from ground sassafras, is a traditional Louisiana Cajun seasoning. It is available in food stores with complete spice assortments.

¼ cup shortening
¾ cup all-purpose flour
¼ pound butter
1 cup finely diced onion
¾ cup finely diced celery
1 medium bell pepper, finely diced
2 medium tomatoes, finely diced
12 cups chicken broth
1 tablespoon fish base
2 teaspoons marjoram
1 teaspoon black pepper
1 teaspoon oregano
½ teaspoon finely diced garlic
¼ cup Worcestershire sauce
1½ tablespoons chicken seasoned stock base
1 teaspoon salt
Dash of cayenne pepper
1 pound fish filets
½ pound fresh okra
2 tablespoons gumbo file
¾ pound cooked baby shrimp

1. First make a roux by melting shortening in skillet over moderate heat and adding flour to form a thick paste. Stirring almost constantly, cook until roux becomes dark brown, 30 to 45 minutes. Remove from heat and let cool.
2. Melt butter in a large pot over medium heat. Add onion, celery, pepper and tomato; sauté until the vegetables turn brown and form a mixture thick enough to hold its shape lightly in a spoon.
3. Add chicken broth, fish base, spices and uncooked fish. Simmer partially covered 45 minutes, making sure the fish is cooked. With a wire whip, beat the soup lightly to separate the fish into small chunks.

4. Add the okra and bring to a boil.
5. Add 6 tablespoons of the roux, stirring constantly until of desired thickness. Add file and cooked shrimp. Serves 6 to 8 generously.

LA QUICHE SPINACH SALAD

2 (10-ounce) bags fresh spinach, washed and stemmed
12 ounces finely diced bacon
1½ cups red wine vinegar
3 tablespoons sugar
3 to 4 dashes Worcestershire sauce
2 dashes salt
1 tablespoon freshly ground pepper
1 cup finely sliced fresh mushrooms

1. Put spinach in bowl and set aside while preparing dressing.
2. Brown bacon until very crisp. Add vinegar, sugar, Worcestershire sauce, salt and pepper. Bring mixture to a boil and let cook down until reduced.
3. Add mushrooms to spinach.
4. Pour dressing over all and toss lightly.

Pat spinach dry before putting in bowl. Salad should be lightly coated with dressing, not soggy and drenched.

CHICKEN MARSALA

6 whole chicken breasts, skinned and deboned
Salt, freshly ground black pepper and Worcestershire sauce
6 tablespoons butter
¼ cup finely chopped red onion
Cognac
Dry Marsala wine
¾ pound fresh mushrooms, sliced
⅓ cup demi-glace or brown sauce
½ cup whipping cream

1. Season each side of double chicken breast with salt, pepper and Worcestershire sauce. Pound out into cutlets about ¼-inch thick.
2. Melt the butter in a skillet and heat until very hot and slightly browned, but do not let it burn.
3. Quickly sear the chicken breasts on both sides in the butter; the inside of the chicken should remain cold. Remove to a platter.
4. Add red onion to the skillet and sauté until light brown.
5. Return chicken to the skillet and flame with Cognac.
6. Add enough Marsala to cover the bottom of the skillet. Remove chicken breasts.
7. Cook mushrooms in demi-glace in the skillet. Taste and correct seasonings.
8. Return chicken to the skillet and cook until done, being very careful not to overcook or chicken will be dry. Remove chicken and reduce the sauce until it thickens enough to hold its shape in a spoon.
9. Stir in cream and spoon sauce over chicken. Each guest is served a whole breast.

Such an exciting entrée should be accompanied by vegetables that enhance its flavor and create a picturesque plate. Broiled tomatoes sprinkled with butter, Parmesan and parsley are very colorful. For a complementary green vegetable, La Quiche suggests young string beans boiled in beef bouillon to which a little dry vermouth has been added. Vegetables should be very crisp. Overcooking ruins flavor and texture. Wild rice is excellent with the chicken.

Be very careful not to overcook chicken or it will be tough. It should feel firm and spring back to the touch.

Brown sauce is an involved preparation. You may use the recipe elsewhere in this book (see index) or buy bottled brown sauce in gourmet departments.

CHEDDAR CHEESE BREAD

¼ pound butter, melted
1 cup buttermilk
2½ cups all-purpose flour
½ teaspoon baking powder
½ teaspoon baking soda
¾ cup sugar
6 ounces Cheddar cheese, grated
1 egg, beaten
¼ cup whole milk

1. In mixing bowl, combine all ingredients except cheese, egg and whole milk. Beat until smooth in electric mixer. Add the cheese and beat until well blended.
2. Grease and flour 2 (8-inch) pie tins.
3. Divide the batter evenly between pans.
4. Bake in 350 degree oven about 50 minutes. Do not overbake.
5. Combine egg and milk and brush the mixture on top of the bread.
6. Return to oven 2 minutes to form a shiny glaze.

When done, the bread should be light golden on top and should spring back when touched. Cut in wedges when it is cool.

LA QUICHE CARROT CAKE

4 eggs
2¼ cups sugar
1¾ cups oil
2¼ cups all-purpose flour
1 tablespoon ground cinnamon
1 teaspoon baking soda
½ teaspoon salt
¾ pound carrots, peeled and grated
Cream Cheese Frosting

1. In a large mixing bowl, place all ingredients except the carrots and frosting and beat with electric mixer until smooth and creamy.
2. Add carrots and beat until smooth.
3. Grease and flour 2 (9-inch) round cake pans. Divide batter between pans.
4. Bake at 350 degrees for 45 minutes. Test for doneness. Cool.
5. Spread with frosting.

Cream Cheese Frosting

4 ounces cream cheese, softened
2 tablespoons butter, softened
2 cups powdered sugar
1 tablespoon vanilla
⅓ cup chopped walnuts
½ cup raisins

1. With electric mixer, whip cream cheese and butter until smooth and creamy.
2. Add sugar, a little at a time
3. Add vanilla, walnuts and raisins and beat until well blended.

Dinner for Four

Stuffed Artichokes with Crabmeat, General Louis Pulaski

Schlumberger Salad

Beef Bourguignon

Brandy Freeze

Wine:

With Artichokes—Meursault 1978
With Beef—Gevrey-Chambertin 1971 or '72

Camille Bermann, Owner
Jesus M. Davila, Executive Chef

At Maxim's food is prepared the Escoffier way using the raw materials of Texas, says the colorful proprietor, Camille Bermann, who boasts that he was Escoffier's last student. He is in the process of turning the reins over to his son Ronnie, who adheres to the same tradition of classic cuisine based on the finest fresh ingredients, handcut meat and fish, freshly prepared sauces and fine wines. Many menu items, such as Red Snapper Pontchartrain and Pompano en Papillote, reflect the senior Bermann's background in Louisiana. He was at the Beverly Country Club in New Orleans before opening the original Maxim's in Houston in 1950.

The restaurant has been in its present downtown location since 1958. A new restaurant is planned in the future in Greenway Plaza. "We have foundation," says Bermann, who worked with Henri Soule at the New York World's Fair in 1939. "About seventy-five percent of my help has been with me for twenty years or more." In traditional fashion, Ronnie apprenticed in France at Fernand Point's La Pyramide and at the Hotel de la Poste in Beaune. He also spent a year learning to make wine at Château Lascombes.

Longtime staff members note that the menu has not changed in their memory except for an addition or two, and it's expected that regular customers will order their favorite dishes, on or off the menu. Some items are named for customers, such as Schlumberger Salad, Stuffed Artichoke with Crabmeat General Louis Pulaski and Veal Sauté à la Jimmie McRae. The wine cellar, setting for many status luncheons and parties, is the joy of connoisseurs for its varied offering of fine vintages.

Crates of fresh fruit and vegetables, looking like still-life paintings, are on display in the entrance of the formal red plush and gilt restaurant. Walls are hung with oversized copies of French impressionist paintings and the owner's many awards, including the coveted gold Escoffier Medal. Fresh flowers center tables set with starched white linens, crystal and silver.

802 Lamar at Milam

STUFFED ARTICHOKES WITH CRABMEAT, GENERAL LOUIS PULASKI

4 artichokes
¼ pound butter
½ cup chopped chives
1 pound crabmeat
1 teaspoon Creole or French mustard
Salt and pepper
¼ cup heavy (whipping) cream
¼ cup dry bread crumbs
Mornay sauce (optional)

1. Wash artichokes. Cut off stems at base and remove small bottom
   leaves. Trim tips of leaves and cut off about ½ inch from top.
   Stand upright in deep saucepan large enough to hold them firmly.
   Add 1 teaspoon salt, 3 inches boiling water and 1 tablespoon lemon
   juice. Cover and boil gently 30 to 45 minutes or until base can be
   pierced easily with fork. If necessary, add more boiling water.
   Remove from pan. Spread leaves gently and remove the thistly choke
   from center with a spoon. Turn artichokes upside down to drain.
2. Sauté chives in melted butter. Add crab. Stir in mustard, salt and
   pepper, cream and bread crumbs; sauté a few minutes until heated
   through. A dash of liquid hot pepper sauce and Worcestershire sauce
   also may be added if desired.
3. Stuff artichokes with crab mixture and serve on individual plates.
   If desired, top with a Mornay sauce.

SCHLUMBERGER SALAD

1½ heads romaine lettuce
2 tomatoes, cut in wedges
1 avocado, peeled, seeded and cut in small pieces
French Dressing
3 hard-cooked eggs, cut in wedges

1. Break up romaine into bite-size pieces.
2. Gently mix lettuce with tomatoes and avocado.
3. Toss lightly with dressing and egg wedges. Serve on chilled plates.

French Dressing

2 tablespoons Creole mustard
3 tablespoons apple cider vinegar
1 clove garlic, finely chopped
1 tablespoon finely chopped celery
1 tablespoon finely chopped chives
¾ cup salad oil
Salt and pepper

1. Combine mustard and vinegar with a fork or whisk.
2. Add chopped garlic, celery and chives.
3. Add oil and salt and pepper to taste. Stir well before mixing
   with salad. Makes about 1 cup.

BEEF BOURGUIGNON

2 pounds beef (loin, butt or lean chuck), cut in cubes
Salt and pepper
Marjoram and thyme to taste (optional)
5 cups good beef stock
1 tablespoon bottled browning sauce
1 tablespoon tomato paste
1 cup dry red wine, such as Burgundy
2 cups fresh mushrooms, sliced or diced
⅓ cup sour cream
Cornstarch
Hot cooked rice

1. Sauté beef cubes until browned in heavy skillet. Sprinkle with desired seasonings.
2. Add stock, browning sauce, tomato paste and wine. Stir well and simmer slowly, covered, 1½ to 2 hours, until beef is tender (chuck will take a little longer). Add more bouillon and wine as necessary to keep beef barely covered.
3. Add mushrooms and simmer about 30 minutes longer.
4. Add sour cream and heat through, but do not boil. Thicken with cornstarch, dissolved in cold water before adding, if needed.
5. Serve on a crown of hot cooked rice.

If desired, (before cooking beef) chop 5 medium onions and cook in oil in skillet until tender. Remove. Return onions to the stew when mushrooms are added.

A nice side dish accompaniment is fresh cut string beans sautéed in butter with tomatoes, seasoning and a little bacon.

BRANDY FREEZE

6 to 8 scoops French vanilla ice cream
French brandy

1. Use 1½ to 2 scoops ice cream and 1 jigger brandy per person.
2. Combine in blender and blend until smooth.
3. Pour into brandy snifters and serve.

This is one of our simplest desserts, but one of the most popular. Use only the best quality French vanilla ice cream and brandy. It's good as an after-dinner drink or as a drink dessert.

Dinner for Four

Queso a la Parrilla

Sopa de Tortilla

Carnitas with Green Sauce, Red Sauce and Guacamole

Flan

Beverage:
Margaritas, Sangria or Mexican Beer

Ninfa Laurenzo, Owner

The growth of Ninfa Laurenzo's empire from one ten-table restaurant near the Houston Ship Channel in 1973 to eight in Houston, San Antonio and Dallas with a multimillion dollar payroll continues to be one of the legends of the restaurant world. In fact, despite the participation of the Laurenzos' daughter and five sons, brothers and sisters-in-law and nieces and nephews, Ninfa's is growing almost faster than the family that runs it.

There's almost always a line at these colorful, casual restaurants adorned with stained glass, tiles and handmade furniture from Mexico City. Ninfa's logo is a bright parrot saying "Gracias." The parrot sets the theme for billboards, the new menu, waiters' name tags, decorations and hospitality because it is a symbol of love and caring.

Ninfa's grew from a small food company making pizza and flour tortillas which she and her husband started in Houston in 1948. After forsaking the food company for the restaurant in 1973, it was Tacos al Carbon—marinated, charbroiled steak served in corn or flour tortillas—which set Ninfa's on its path to fame. They are now trademarked Tacos a la Ninfa. Other stellar menu items are the Margaritas, the red and green sauces, Queso a la Parrilla (a melted white cheese, mushroom, pepper and onion dish Parrilla-style) and flautas (deep-fried beef or chicken tacos with guacamole and sour cream). Many off-the-menu items are equally famous.

The food is a combination of dishes prepared from time-proven home and family recipes, many from Ninfa's mother, and others discovered while traveling in Mexico—"real Mexican food, not Tex-Mex," says Ninfa. She believes in using only fresh top-quality products. Sauces are made fresh two or three times a day. "We make everything from tortillas to chorizo and everything is cooked fresh daily." Flour tortillas are still painstakingly made, one by one, by hand.

2704 Navigation
6154 Westheimer
9333-B Katy Freeway (Echo Lane)
8507 Gulf Freeway
231 Bammel
Richmond at Kirby Drive

QUESO A LA PARRILLA

4 tablespoons butter
½ cup chopped onion
¼ cup chopped bell pepper
¼ cup chopped mushrooms
2 cups shredded Queso Chihuahua
Flour tortillas

1. In pan or oval skillet melt butter and sauté onion, bell pepper and mushrooms about 5 minutes.
2. Add cheese and stir until melted.
3. Place under broiler until browned on top, but don't let burn.
4. Serve with flour tortillas.

Queso Chihuahua is a white goat cheese from Mexico and may be difficult to find. Monterey jack or mozzarella may be substituted, although the Mexican cheese is preferable.

SOPA DE TORTILLA
(Tortilla Soup)

1 (8-ounce) can tomatoes
1 medium onion, cut up
1 clove garlic
1 tablespoon snipped cilantro or chopped parsley
¼ teaspoon sugar
4 cups chicken broth
6 (6-inch) corn tortillas
Oil
1 cup (¼ pound) shredded Monterey Jack or longhorn cheese

1. In a blender container, combine undrained tomatoes, onion, garlic, cilantro and sugar. Cover and blend until nearly smooth. Turn into a large saucepan; stir in chicken broth. Bring to a boil, cover and simmer 20 minutes.
2. Cut tortillas into ½-inch wide strips. Fry in ½ inch hot oil 45 to 50 seconds or until crisp and lightly browned. Drain on paper towels.
3. Divide fried tortilla strips and cheese among soup bowls. Ladle soup over. Serve immediately.

Cilantro may be found in Mexican markets and in many supermarket produce sections. It is sometimes called fresh coriander or Chinese parsley.

CARNITAS WITH GREEN SAUCE, RED SAUCE AND GUACAMOLE

1½ to 2 pounds boneless pork shoulder
Garlic salt and pepper
Romaine
Tomato slices
Avocado slices
Fresh onion rings
Green Sauce
Red Sauce
Guacamole
Sour Cream
Warm corn or flour tortillas

1. Preheat oven to 350 degrees.
2. Cut pork into 2-inch chunks and spread in a 12x7x2-inch baking
   pan. Sprinkle lightly with garlic salt and pepper.
3. Add water to a depth of 1 inch. Bake in preheated oven 2 to 2½
   hours or until water evaporates and meat is brown.
4. Serve on a bed of romaine flanked by avocado and tomato slices. Top
   with white onion rings and serve with sauces and sour cream. Wrap
   in tortillas to eat.

Ninfa's Green Sauce

1 ripe (soft to the touch) avocado
¼ cup sour cream
¼ cup milk
1 teaspoon minced onion
1 clove garlic, mashed to a pulp with ¼ teaspoon salt
1 tablespoon minced fresh cilantro or ¼ teaspoon dried cilantro
½ teaspoon hot pepper sauce (or to taste)
2 to 3 tablespoons fresh lemon juice

1. Peel avocado and mash to a smooth pulp.
2. Add sour cream, milk, onion, garlic, cilantro, pepper sauce and
   lemon juice and blend with a wire whip.
3. Let stand at least an hour before serving. Refrigerate any leftover
   sauce.

Ninfa's Red Sauce

5 tomatoes
1 teaspoon salt
2 arbol chilies, fried in oil
2 serrano chilies
1 tablespoon chopped cilantro
½ teaspoon chopped garlic

1. Boil tomatoes until tender in a small amount of water. Remove from heat and place in blender.
2. Add salt, chilies, cilantro and garlic and blend to the desired consistency. This should be a thick, delicious sauce.

Arbol chilies are long (about 2½ inches), brilliant red chilies with smooth, shiny skin, and have a real bite. Serranos are small (about 1½ inches) tapered green chilies usually only available canned. Although tiny, they too have a bite. They are available at Mexican markets and sometimes at the Farmers Co-op Market. If not available, substitute any small very hot chile for the arbol and jalapeños for the serranos.

Guacamole

2 medium avocados, seeded, peeled and cut up
½ small onion, cut up
2 tablespoons lemon juice
1 clove garlic, minced
½ teaspoon salt
¼ teaspoon pepper

1. Place cut-up avocados in blender container with onion, lemon juice, garlic, salt and pepper.
2. Cover and blend until well combined. Makes about 1¼ cups.

Use this as a dip for chips or as a sauce with a main dish.

FLAN

1¾ cups sugar
8 eggs
2 tall (13-ounce) cans evaporated milk
2 teaspoons vanilla

1. Place 1 cup sugar in a deep pan in which the custard is to be baked and place over heat. Stir constantly until the sugar melts and turns golden. Tip the pan around until it is entirely coated with the caramel. Let cool while making the custard.
2. Beat eggs; add milk, remaining sugar and vanilla. Mix well. Strain into the caramel-coated pan, cover and place pan in a larger pan containing hot water up to about 1 inch from the top of the flan pan.
3. Bake at 350 degrees 1 hour or until a knife inserted in the center comes out clean. Cool custard, then refrigerate.
4. Before unmolding, check to see that the caramel isn't hardened so that it will interfere with unmolding. The flan should move around easily as you tip the mold. If it doesn't, dip the mold in a pan of warm water for about 5 minutes, then test again. When ready to serve, turn out on platter, pour brandy or rum over the flan, ignite with a taper and take to the table flaming. Serves 8 to 10.

Flan is best when made several hours before serving and when thoroughly chilled. It may also be made in custard cups. You can also caramelize the sugar in a heavy skillet or saucepan, then pour into a glass baking dish, tipping so the caramel covers the dish evenly. Be sure to let caramel cool thoroughly before pouring custard over it.

Dinner for Four

Crab Claws Lamonte

Fried Zucchini and Cauliflower

Minestrone with Miniature Meatballs

Beef Steak alla Nino

Sfingis

Wine:

With Crab and Zucchini—Orvieto Secco
With Soup and Steak—Barolo Bersano

Vincent Mandola, Owner-Chef

"We're doing down-home-style family cooking," says native Houstonian Vincent Mandola of Nino's, who opened the restaurant as a family endeavor with his brother Tony in 1977. (They are also brothers of one of the owners of D'Amico's.)

"We wanted something comfortable, not a fancy spot," says Mandola. With the help of their wives, Mary Virginia and Phyllis, they cleaned and renovated a storefront building on the fringe of downtown which had been a grocery store plus living quarters in the '30s. The restaurant is named for Mandola's father, whose picture hangs on the wall and appears on the menu cover. Many of the recipes come from their mother, Grace Mandola.

Fans quickly spread the word on Nino's deep-fried vegetable appetizers, pizza and handmade ravioli. The menu has since been expanded with several veal dishes, Chicken Oliva (liberally bathed in olive oil and garlic), barbecued shrimp, Crab Claws Lamonte (inspired and named by a cousin in Dallas), seafood, pasta dishes and Mama Grace's own minestrone.

Now wholly owned by Vincent, who is also the chef, the restaurant was recently enlarged to include a bar area. An antique bar from an old Houston tavern is its focal point. Natural wood floor, dark wood tables, ceiling fans, palms and lace-trimmed curtains provide atmosphere.

In the informal dining room there are lots of plants and bright kelly green accents on menu covers, cafe drapes, accessories and staff aprons. Calligraphy for the distinctive menus was done by Bobette Chapman.

2817 West Dallas

CRAB CLAWS LAMONTE

4 cloves garlic, finely chopped
1 green onion, finely chopped
½ teaspoon oregano
¼ pound melted butter
½ pound crab claws
½ teaspoon ground black pepper

1. Sauté garlic, green onion and oregano in saucepan in melted butter 2 minutes.
2. Add crab claws and sauté. Sprinkle with pepper. Stir gently until crab is heated through.
3. Serve on small platter and dip crab claws in butter remaining from cooking as a sauce.

Use fairly small crab claws, about 15 to 20 for four people. Remove three-fourths of the shell to reveal the meaty part of claw.

FRIED ZUCCHINI AND CAULIFLOWER

1 cup flour
3 beaten eggs
1 cup milk
1 cup fine dry bread crumbs
½ teaspoon salt
½ teaspoon white pepper
½ teaspoon oregano
2 zucchini, sliced ¼-inch thick
1 medium cauliflower, separated into florets and blanched
Vegetable oil
Lemon Butter

1. Place 3 shallow pans side by side with flour in the first, beaten egg and milk in the second and combined bread crumbs, salt, pepper and oregano in the third.
2. Dust zucchini completely with flour. Be sure cauliflower is done, but firm, and well drained. Dust completely with flour; shake off excess.
3. Dip zucchini and cauliflower in egg wash, being sure pieces are completely covered.
4. Roll in seasoned bread crumbs.
5. Deep fry in hot oil until golden brown. Serve in a basket with **Lemon Butter** on the side.

Lemon Butter

Add the juice of half a lemon to ¼ to ½ cup melted butter.

Oil should be about 350 degrees for frying. To test for proper temperature, drop in a piece of the zucchini; it should cook within three minutes. Don't add too much at one time when cooking or temperature of the oil will be lowered and vegetables will be soggy and absorb grease.

MINESTRONE WITH MINIATURE MEATBALLS

1 small stalk celery (whole celery)
1 yellow onion
2 carrots
2 zucchini
2 small meaty stock bones
2 cups heavy-style tomato sauce
Water
Salt and black pepper to taste
Miniature Meatballs

1. Clean and dice all vegetables.
2. Add to medium size stock pot and cover with water.
3. Add bones, tomato sauce and salt and pepper to taste.
4. Bring to a boil. Let simmer about 1 hour. While soup is cooking, prepare meatballs.
5. Add meatballs to soup and simmer 10 minutes.
6. Serve in bowls and divide meatballs among servings.

Miniature Meatballs

4 sprigs parsley, finely chopped
1 green onion, finely chopped
¼ teaspoon salt
½ teaspoon pepper
1 tablespoon bread crumbs
1 egg
¼ cup grated Romano cheese
½ pound ground beef

1. Add parsley, green onion, salt, pepper, bread crumbs, egg and cheese to beef. Mix well.
2. Roll small portions into miniature meatballs about ½ inch in diameter.
3. Add to soup and simmer 10 minutes.
4. Serve in bowls and divide meatballs among servings.

BEEF STEAK ALLA NINO

4 (10-ounce) New York strip steaks
Salt and black pepper
Olive oil
¼ pound butter
1 small yellow onion, sliced ½-inch thick
1 medium bell pepper, sliced ½-inch thick
4 medium mushrooms, thinly sliced
4 strips pimiento
½ cup dry red wine such as Bardolino or Valpolicella

1. Salt and pepper steaks.
2. Cover bottom of a large skillet with olive oil and heat over medium heat.
3. Lay steaks in the skillet and sear very well on one side. Turn and cook to desired doneness. Remove steaks from pan.
4. Drain oil and add butter to pan.
5. Sauté onion, bell pepper, mushrooms and pimiento in melted butter. When vegetables are done, but are still firm, return steaks to skillet.
6. Add wine and simmer until wine evaporates. Arrange steaks on platter and cover with sautéed vegetables to serve.

Steaks should have some fat marbling for flavor. Use a light Italian olive oil and be sure the oil is hot before steaks are started. Steak should be turned only once, and with tongs rather than a fork that pierces the meat. Vegetables should be sautéed tender-crisp.

SFINGIS

1 cup all-purpose flour
½ teaspoon ground nutmeg
½ teaspoon cinnamon
1 level tablespoon baking powder
1 egg
¼ cup sugar
¾ cup milk, or more if needed
Powdered sugar
Honey

1. Combine flour, nutmeg, cinnamon and baking powder and sift into a large bowl.
2. Beat egg and slowly add sugar, beating constantly. Stir in milk. Add to dry ingredients and stir until well blended. You should have a smooth, medium-thick batter. Add more milk if needed.
3. Drop batter by the tablespoon into deep hot (350 to 375-degree) oil and turn repeatedly for even browning. Remove with a slotted spoon.
4. Sprinkle with powdered sugar.
5. Serve with honey on the side in a saucer or small bowl for dipping.

Sfingis are Italian drop doughnuts and are typical of the area in the south of Italy where Mandola's family originally came from.

RAINBOW LODGE

Dinner for Six

Rainbow Salad

Cream of Cucumber Soup

Fresh Gulf Trout with Brown Butter Sauce

Fresh Asparagus with Hollandaise

Yellow Squash

Walnut Pie

Wine:
With Soup—Château Montelena Chardonnay 1978
With Fish—Chevalier Montrachet 1975

Max Yarbrough, Owner
Jim Alexander, General Manager
Trond Haugvoll, Executive Chef

Somewhere over the treetops are Houston's steel and glass skyscrapers, but at the Rainbow Lodge, less than 10 minutes from downtown, you'll think you've been transported to a rustic hunting lodge.

Built as a private one-story residence in early 1935, the house was completely flooded by Buffalo Bayou later that year. The second owner, a doctor, added the second and third stories and enclosed the ground level, which is now the kitchen. Max Yarbrough found the house in 1976, remodeled it and furnished it with an eclectic mix of antiques and quaint memorabilia. He retained the pleasing hodgepodge of rustic purple cedar tree-trunk railings, antiques, polished floors, dark paneling and gaslight ambiance while expanding the back in multi-level contemporary style.

The former master bedroom on the third floor is now an elegant private dining room with its own fireplace and balcony. Some of the ornate gold leaf sofas and chairs in the cocktail area are from a 20th Century-Fox inventory for a 1926 production of "Annie Get Your Gun." The two-story glass walls at the back reveal scenic views of the bayou, a small lake with waterfalls and grounds populated by a zoo of whimsical topiaries in animal shapes. An adventurous raccoon family wanders up on the patio from time to time.

It's a house for all seasons and weathers, but since the gazebo near the lake has become such a popular place for weddings and receptions, most romantics hope for sunshine. Others feel that Rainbow Lodge is at its romantic best when it rains.

"I want all who visit Rainbow Lodge to feel as if they were in their own homes," says Yarbrough. "My desire is to offer guests the freshest foods prepared with the utmost care and served in a friendly and attentive manner."

No. 1 Birdsall off Memorial

RAINBOW SALAD
(Ratatouille, Tabouli and Marinated Vegetables)

Ratatouille

¼ cup oil (half may be olive oil if desired)
2 bell peppers, chopped
1 cup thinly sliced onions
1 clove garlic, finely minced
1 teaspoon oregano
1 teaspoon salt
¼ teaspoon cayenne
½ teaspoon basil
¼ teaspoon thyme
½ bay leaf
½ cup dry white wine
1 medium eggplant, peeled and chopped
½ pound fresh mushrooms
3 medium zucchini, chopped
1 cup tomato paste
4 tomatoes, peeled and chopped

1. Heat oil in medium size saucepan to very hot. Add chopped bell pepper, onion and garlic and sauté 2 to 3 minutes.
2. Add oregano, salt, cayenne, basil, thyme and bay leaf.
3. Add white wine and chopped eggplant. Mix well.
4. Add mushrooms, zucchini, tomato paste and tomatoes. Stir thoroughly and cook over medium-low heat 1 hour. Stir often. Use additional tomato paste to color or thicken to taste. Chill.

Tabouli

1 clove garlic, diced
1 teaspoon salt
1 teaspoon white pepper
1 teaspoon cayenne
1 cup water
2 cups tabouli (cracked bulgar wheat)
3 green onions, chopped
¼ bunch fresh parsley, chopped fine
1 tomato, diced
¼ head red cabbage, finely diced
¼ cup lemon juice
2 tablespoons olive oil

1. Add garlic, salt, pepper and cayenne to water in a medium-size saucepan. Bring to a full boil with tabouli. Cover.
2. Set aside and let cool before adding remaining ingredients.
3. Chill.

Marinated Vegetables

¾ head cauliflower, cut in florets
¾ bunch broccoli, cut in florets
¾ pound carrots, peeled and sliced
¾ pound green squash such as zucchini
1 onion, thinly sliced
¼ cup honey
1 cup herb dressing

1. Steam cut vegetables lightly (except onion). Drain and place in a shallow pan. Top with onion.
2. Add honey and herb dressing. Add water for desired consistency.
3. Chill.

To serve:

After **Ratatouille, Tabouli** and **Marinated Vegetables** are chilled, arrange equal portions on a plate. A bed of lettuce is optional, but makes an attractive presentation.

CREAM OF CUCUMBER SOUP

4 cups diced cucumber which has been peeled and seeded
5 cups chicken stock
5 tablespoons butter
4 tablespoons flour
3 cups light cream
1 teaspoon salt
½ teaspoon white pepper
¼ teaspoon tarragon
½ teaspoon ground dill weed
½ cup sour cream

1. Place cucumbers in a saucepan with 3 cups of the chicken stock. Cook over medium heat until the cucumber is tender.
2. Reserve ½ cup of the cooked cucumber for garnish. In a blender, purée the remaining cucumber with the stock in which it was cooked.
3. In a soup kettle, melt butter. Blend in flour, light cream and spices.
4. Over low heat, stir 3 minutes. Add puréed cucumber and remaining 2 cups chicken stock. Cook 3 more minutes. Whip in sour cream just before serving. Adjust seasonings to taste.
5. Serve hot or cold. If serving cold, place soup in a smaller bowl placed on top of a bed of ice. Garnish with the remaining cucumber.

Skim chicken broth well so soup will be light and delicate in texture.

A thinly sliced whole cucumber may be substituted for the garnish. Other fresh vegetables such as carrots, celery and squash make nice garnishes, too. A bit of cayenne spices up the cold soup nicely.

FRESH GULF TROUT WITH BROWN BUTTER SAUCE

6 fresh Gulf trout filets
1 cup flour
2 teaspoons salt
¾ teaspoon white pepper
4 eggs, beaten
Melted butter

1. Dredge fish in flour seasoned with salt and pepper.
2. Roll filets in beaten eggs.

continued

3. Place fish in a hot skillet with enough melted butter to cover bottom and sauté until light brown. Transfer fish to 350-degree oven 5 more minutes.
4. Place filets on individual plates and top with **Brown Butter Sauce.**

Brown Butter Sauce

4 tablespoons butter
4 tablespoons flour
Fish stock or chicken broth (about 1 cup)
¼ teaspoon white pepper
¼ teaspoon salt
½ cup white wine
2 large tablespoons butter
¾ cup whipping cream
Juice of 1 lemon

1. Brown butter and add flour. Let bubble and simmer to a roux, a thick dark mixture. Add fish stock until sauce reaches a medium consistency.
2. Add pepper, salt, white wine and 2 large tablespoons of butter.
3. Stir in whipping cream and lemon juice and simmer, stirring, until smooth.

FRESH ASPARAGUS WITH HOLLANDAISE

Cook asparagus in a large deep pan with steamer rack. Be sure water is boiling before putting the asparagus in the steamer. It takes 5 minutes or so for 10 to 12 spears. Test in the middle of the spear for doneness. At Rainbow Lodge we steam the minimum time, then drop the asparagus into ice water in a colander to keep it crisp. Reheat very briefly in the hot cooking water before serving.

1 to 1½ pounds fresh asparagus of uniform size
Hollandaise Sauce

1. Trim tough ends of asparagus.
2. Steam 10 to 15 minutes. Be careful not to overcook.
3. Serve topped with **Hollandaise Sauce.**

Hollandaise Sauce

¼ pound butter
2 egg yolks, slightly beaten
1 tablespoon lemon juice
Dash of cayenne

1. Divide butter in 2 equal parts. Put half in the top of a double
   boiler and combine with egg yolks and lemon juice. Cook, stirring
   constantly, over boiling water. To prevent curdling, do not let
   boiling water touch bottom of pan until butter is melted.
2. Beat in remaining butter with a whisk and stir until thick and smooth.
3. Remove double boiler and place in cold water to stop cooking.
4. Stir in cayenne.

YELLOW SQUASH

6 yellow squash
Butter
Salt and pepper

1. Lightly steam yellow squash. Slice in half lengthwise and sauté
   in melted butter 1 minute.
2. Remove squash from butter and season lightly with salt and
   pepper before serving.

WALNUT PIE

1 cup light corn syrup
1 cup dark brown sugar
⅓ cup flour
¼ teaspoon salt
1 teaspoon vanilla extract
1 teaspoon brandy extract
1 teaspoon rum extract
3 eggs, beaten
4 tablespoons melted butter
1 cup walnut halves
1 unbaked 9-inch pie shell

1. In mixing bowl, combine corn syrup, sugar, flour, salt and extracts.
2. Mix well, then add eggs one at a time. Beat until completely
   combined.
3. Add butter and mix.
4. Pour into pie shell. Top with walnut halves and bake 40 minutes
   at 350 degrees, or until set.

the RIVOLI

Dinner for Four

Gazpacho

Spinach and Watercress Salad with Pine Nuts

Stuffed Dover Sole Zielinsky

Grand Marnier Ice Parfait

Wine:

*With Gazpacho and Salad—Clos du Bois Chardonnay
1978
With Sole—Chassagne-Montrachet 1978*

*Willie Rometsch and Ed Zielinsky, Owners
Gunther Hoffman, Executive Chef
Pierre Gutknecht, Sous Chef*

The Rivoli is one of Houston's favorite places to see and be seen. Celebrities such as Tom Jones, Rock Hudson and authors Tommy Thompson and Truman Capote come for the impeccably prepared cuisine and the comfortable, stylish ambiance; others can't be blamed for considering a bit of elbow-rubbing among the restaurant's attractions. Opened only a few years ago, the Rivoli is rapidly acquiring a reputation as an internationally fashionable dining spot.

Palms and latticework—reflected in mirror-accented walls—emphasize a garden atmosphere, while towering silk flower arrangements and David Adickes paintings bring out an inherent elegance in the decor. Not long ago the kitchen, bar and dining areas were expanded, at which time an intimate piano room was created next to the Garden Room. Private parties may be accommodated in the Wine Room.

The menu has a Continental character, leaning heavily to veal, fresh fish and other seafood. Many meat entrées also feature seafood, such as Tournedos St. Grimmod, topped with charcoal broiled shrimp, and Tournedos Nizza and Veal Filet Oskar, both of which are topped with King crab meat. The Calves' Liver Veronique is a favorite of the many business executives from the nearby Galleria and Greenway Plaza areas who deal over lunch at the Rivoli. The menu, which also features quail and frog legs, caters mainly to a sophisticated, well-traveled clientele, according to co-owners Willie Rometsch and Ed Zielinsky.

Rometsch, a European-trained chef and restaurant entrepreneur, has pioneered several "restaurant rows" and helped to establish eleven of Houston's most successful restaurants. He also has an interest in the new Wentletrap Restaurant in Galveston. Zielinsky comes to us from New York where he owned the Grenadier and was associated with several successful clubs, including the well-known Raffles.

5636 Richmond

GAZPACHO

3 large tomatoes, peeled and finely chopped
2 cucumbers, peeled, seeded and chopped
1 bell pepper, seeded and chopped
1 clove garlic, chopped
3 ounces roasted sliced almonds
10 ounces beef consommé
10 ounces tomato juice
Salt and pepper
Fresh lemon juice
Liquid hot pepper sauce
Pinch of cumin

1. Combine chopped vegetables and almonds.
2. Combine consommé, tomato juice, salt and pepper to taste,
   lemon juice, pepper sauce and cumin to taste and add to vegetables.
3. Chill for 2 to 3 hours. Serve in chilled cups and garnish with cucumber.

SPINACH AND WATERCRESS SALAD WITH PINE NUTS

1½ to 2 bunches fresh spinach, stems trimmed
1½ to 2 bunches watercress
Dressing
4 ounces pine nuts (pignolia), lightly sautéed in butter
4 or 8 cherry tomatoes

1. Clean and trim spinach and watercress, wash and drain well.
   Pat dry. Tear into bite-sized pieces.
2. Place in a bowl and mix gently, but thoroughly, with dressing.
3. Arrange on chilled salad plates, sprinkle with pine nuts and garnish
   with cherry tomatoes.

Dressing

4 tablespoons prepared mustard
1 tablespoon dry English mustard (Colman's)
½ cup white vinegar
¾ cup walnut oil
Dash of oregano
Salt and pepper to taste

1. Combine mustards, vinegar and oil and whisk together.
2. Season to taste with oregano, salt and pepper.

*Walnut oil is cold pressed and has a delicate but discernible nutty
flavor. It gives an intriguing and elegant quality to salads.*

STUFFED DOVER SOLE ZIELINSKY

4 Dover sole, skinned and cleaned
Salt, pepper and flour
Oil and butter
Stuffing
Brown butter (see note below)
Chopped fresh parsley
Paprika

1. Season fish with salt and pepper and dust with flour.
2. Sauté in fry pan in equal parts of oil and melted butter, about
   ¼ cup in all.
3. Remove bones and stuff fish.
4. Top with brown butter and chopped parsley. Garnish with the
   bone dusted with paprika.

*Brown butter is made by cooking butter to a dark brown color without
letting it burn. In classic preparation, you would add about 3 tablespoons
chopped parsley and 1 tablespoon capers to 10 tablespoons butter, then
just before serving add a tablespoon of vinegar heated in the same pan.*

Stuffing

1 pound King crabmeat
Butter
1 green onion, chopped
¼ cup sliced mushrooms
3 artichoke bottoms, sliced
1½ tablespoons flour
Chablis
¼ cup whipping cream
Salt and pepper
Lemon juice

1. Sauté crabmeat in melted butter with the green onion, mushrooms
   and artichokes.
2. Dust with flour, stir and add a splash of Chablis.
3. Stir in the cream and bring just to a boil.
4. Season with salt, pepper and lemon juice and heat through.

Real Dover sole is not always easy to find, and since it is a flatfish, it must be handled delicately. To skin: Lay fish on cutting board, eyes up. Slit skin along the fin line close to the fins. Cut across the skin at the tail and loosen enough with a knife to grasp skin. It is slippery, and it may help to wrap a paper or cloth towel around it. Pull skin off toward the head. After fish is cooked, it is easy to remove the bones. Dover sole has four filets, two on each side, which are clearly divided by the bone. At the Rivoli we dust the bone with paprika and use as a garnish.

GRAND MARNIER ICE PARFAIT

5 egg yolks
2 whole eggs
½ pound (1¼ cups) powdered sugar
1 envelope unflavored gelatin
½ teaspoon vanilla extract
3 cups whipping cream
½ cup Grand Marnier
Whipped cream and chocolate chips for garnish

1. Put a foil collar around a 1-quart soufflé dish.
2. Whip eggs lightly to blend. Add sugar gradually to prevent lumping. Cook in a double boiler over simmering water until mixture begins to thicken, about 5 minutes, whisking constantly. Remove top of double boiler from heat and continue whisking mixture as it cools.
3. Soften gelatin in ¼ cup cold water, place over medium heat and stir until completely dissolved. Whisk into the eggs to blend thoroughly.
4. Stir in vanilla.
5. Whip the cream and combine with Grand Marnier. Fold into the egg mixture.
6. Spoon into prepared soufflé dish and freeze overnight.
7. Remove the collar and cover the parfait with whipped cream. Sprinkle with chocolate chips.
8. To serve: spoon onto dessert plates.

If desired, reserve a half cup of the three cups whipping cream to use as the garnish. A delicious variation is to substitute Amaretto for the Grand Marnier and garnish with whipped cream and sliced almonds.

Rotisserie
for
Beef and Bird

Dinner for Four

Avocado with Baby Shrimp

Onion Soup Gratinée with Calvados

Roast Duckling à l'Orange

Zucchini Casserole with Sour Cream

Yeast Rolls

Bread Pudding with Hot Whiskey Sauce

Wine:

With Appetizer—Château de Puligny-Montrachet 1977
With Duck—Hermitage M. Chapoutier 1976
After Dinner—Armagnac

Joe and Gigi Mannke, Owners
Joe Mannke, Chef

Located on what some call Houston's Far West Frontier, the Rotisserie for Beef and Bird is a celebration of the bounty of America. The brick-hearthed rotisserie dominates the dining room and the menu reflects an America-the-Plentiful theme. It's only natural that Thanksgiving is the highlight of the year, but there are always generous servings of fresh seafood, aged beef, farm-fresh vegetables, home-baked bread, jams and desserts.

The restaurant is owned by Joe Mannke, a classically trained chef and former food and beverage director of the Hyatt Regency. He earned his stripes in the kitchens of several internationally known hotels and as the chef in charge of Disney World's seven kitchens when it opened. There they served more than 10,000 meals a day. Mannke is a member of the American Academy of Chefs, Confrerie de la Chain Rotisseurs and Les Amis d'Escoffier.

"At the Rotisserie, we are going back to the basics—beautiful fresh food, the traditional technique of cooking on the rotisserie as settlers did centuries ago, and old-style Texas hospitality." The restaurant also boasts a lengthy and varied list of fairly priced wines.

Earlier in his career Mannke was executive chef for Anthony's Pier 4 in Boston, which, during his tenure, became the largest-volume restaurant in the United States. The Rotisserie reflects his fondness for New England in its clean-lined Cape Cod architecture and furnishings.

The solid parquet oak table tops were handmade by a southern California wood-carving family. Captain's chairs are upholstered in rich burgundy and dark olive. Solid brass stagecoach lamps define the windows, and at the entrance to the dining room a cast iron stove (the Majestic Company's finest in 1930) displays such heritage desserts as oversized apple pie and rippled chocolate fudge cake.

2200 Wilcrest

AVOCADO WITH BABY SHRIMP

¾ pound baby shrimp
2 ounces (4 tablespoons) chopped peanuts
1 rib celery, chopped
2 ounces canned or fresh pineapple, chopped
5 ounces (about ¾ cup) mayonnaise
1 ounce (about 2 tablespoons) tomato ketchup
4 lettuce leaves
2 large ripe avocados, peeled and seeds removed
Hard-cooked egg, cucumber slices and tomato wedges for garnish

1. In a mixing bowl, combine shrimp, peanuts, celery, pineapple, mayonnaise and ketchup.
2. On individual plates, arrange a lettuce leaf and half an avocado. Fill with shrimp mixture in the center.
3. Garnish with quartered egg, cucumber slices and tomato wedges.

ONION SOUP GRATINEE WITH CALVADOS

2 medium onions, thinly sliced
2 tablespoons butter
½ teaspoon thyme
4½ cups beef broth
Salt and pepper
1½ ounces Calvados (applejack)
8 thinly sliced triangles of toasted bread
½ cup diced mozzarella cheese

1. Sauté onion slices in butter in heavy skillet until lightly colored. Add thyme and broth. Season to taste with salt and pepper and simmer over low heat 20 minutes.
2. Preheat oven to 450 degrees.
3. Add Calvados to soup and pour into 4 individual heatproof bowls.
4. Top with toast triangles, sprinkle with mozzarella and bake until golden brown, 5 to 7 minutes.

Onions are one of the oldest foods in our civilization. Even Alexander the Great brought onions from Egypt to Greece and fed them to his troops. The mozzarella is the best cheese for the soup, I think, because it browns much better and develops a desirable stringiness. It is diced rather than grated, because mozzarella is hard to grate properly.

ROAST DUCKLING A L'ORANGE

2 ducklings
1 teaspoon salt
$\frac{1}{8}$ teaspoon black pepper
$\frac{1}{2}$ teaspoon rosemary
1 rib celery, chopped
1 small carrot, chopped
1 small onion, chopped
2 tablespoons flour
3 cups hot water
Orange Sauce
Orange wedges and fresh watercress for garnish

1. Preheat oven to 450 degrees.
2. Trim ducklings of excess fat at the base of the tail and inside. Chop giblets.
3. Season well inside and out with salt, pepper and rosemary.
4. Place ducklings and chopped giblets in a pan and roast in preheated oven 1½ hours. Baste from time to time. Remove ducklings and keep warm.
5. Pour off all but 2 tablespoons fat from the roasting pan, add the chopped vegetables and sauté 10 minutes, stirring constantly. Dust with the flour and combine with hot water. Boil 15 minutes, then strain.
6. Make **Orange Sauce.**
7. Cut the ducks in quarters. Garnish with the orange wedges and fresh watercress. Serve sauce on the side.

Orange Sauce

3 tablespoons sugar
1 tablespoon butter
1 orange, cut in wedges
½ cup cider vinegar
1 cup orange juice
3 cloves
1 teaspoon English mustard
½ cup Grand Marnier liqueur

1. Melt sugar and butter together in a saucepan. Add the orange wedges and the vinegar and bring to a boil.
2. Pour in the basic sauce from the duck and add the orange juice, cloves and mustard. Boil 5 minutes.
3. Strain and combine with the Grand Marnier.

ZUCCHINI CASSEROLE WITH SOUR CREAM

2 pounds zucchini, sliced
¼ pound butter
½ cup sour cream
4 slices American cheese, chopped
½ teaspoon salt
⅛ teaspoon paprika
1 egg yolk, beaten
1 tablespoon chopped chives
½ cup Ritz cracker crumbs

1. Cook zucchini 2 minutes in boiling water; drain and place in a greased 1½ or 2-quart baking dish.
2. Meanwhile, melt butter. Combine half of the melted butter with sour cream, cheese, salt and paprika. Simmer over low heat, stirring constantly, until cheese is melted.
3. Remove from heat. Pour a little of the hot sauce into the egg yolk and whisk to combine to temper the egg yolk gradually. Return mixture to the hot sauce and whisk until smooth. Add chives.
4. Toss cracker crumbs with remaining melted butter and sprinkle over zucchini.
5. Bake in moderate (350-degree) oven 20 minutes. Serves 4 to 6.

YEAST ROLLS

Makes 18 rolls

6 cups unbleached all-purpose flour
1 tablespoon salt
¼ cup sugar
3½ cups warm water (110 degrees)
1 package active dry yeast
2 tablespoons vegetable shortening

1. Preheat oven to 375 degrees.
2. Sift flour, salt and sugar together in a mixing bowl.
3. Dissolve yeast in 1 cup of the warm water. Make a well in the center of the flour and pour yeast into it. Add remaining water and shortening, a little at a time, and work the dough until it leaves the sides of the bowl clean.
4. Turn dough out on a lightly floured surface and knead it 10 minutes. Set aside to rise in a bowl in a warm place until it has doubled in size.
5. Divide dough into 18 portions, form into rolls and place on a baking sheet.
6. Dust tops of rolls with flour and let rise again.
7. Bake in preheated oven for 30 minutes or until golden brown.

BREAD PUDDING WITH HOT WHISKEY SAUCE

5 (½-inch thick) slices French bread
3 tablespoons butter
3 egg whites
½ cup sugar
1 ounce dark rum
2 cups milk
½ cup cream
½ teaspoon vanilla extract
Hot Whiskey Sauce

1. Preheat oven to 375 degrees.
2. Butter each slice of bread and arrange in a 2-quart baking dish, buttered side up.
3. Beat egg whites, sugar and rum.
4. In a saucepan, bring the milk and cream to a boil. Combine with egg mixture, add vanilla and strain over the bread.

5. Set dish in a roasting pan filled with water to within an inch of the top of the baking dish and bake in preheated oven for 45 minutes.
6. Serve with **Hot Whiskey Sauce.**

Hot Whiskey Sauce

1 quart milk
6 egg yolks
¼ cup bourbon
½ cup sugar
1 teaspoon cornstarch

1. Bring milk to a boil.
2. Whip egg yolks, bourbon, sugar and cornstarch together and combine with the hot milk.
3. Simmer, but do not boil, 5 minutes.
4. Serve with **Bread Pudding.**

Rudi's . . .

Dinner for Four

Sautéed Artichokes Pauline

Chicken Egg-Drop Soup

Pine Nut Salad Pearce

Veal Lucero

Fettuccine Alfredo

Steamed Fresh Broccoli

Amaretto Freeze

Wine:
With Artichokes, Soup and Salad—Ockfener Bockstein
1976
With Veal—Puligny-Montrachet 1976
After Dessert—Domaine Chandon Brut

Joe Lucia, Owner
Joe Lucia Jr., Manager
Denny Dorsch, Executive Chef

Tall, stately entrance doors, a veritable sculpture of handwrought silver, copper and brass by Thom Wheeler, set the sophisticated scene at Rudi's. The rich, soothing decor is a mix of cordovan-colored suede walls and banquettes, burgundy carpet, leather chairs and arched niches holding brass containers of stylized flowers and leaves.

Devoted fans of Rudi's have almost written the menu for this Continental restaurant which has strong Italian leanings. Although the menu changes seasonally to offer such delicacies as softshell crab, many customers insist that some things stay the same. The assorted seafood appetizer, Tomatoes Nicoise, Veal Piccata and Cannelloni are perennial favorites. Some items have been added as re-creations of dishes customers have enjoyed on their travels. Other recipes, including the Artichokes Pauline, came from Lucia's family.

Emphasis is on simple preparations that play up the quality of the food. Sauces tend to be the classics. "We spare no expense in getting the finest quality ingredients because our customers expect quality and consistency," says Chef Denny Dorsch.

Lucia bought the restaurant in 1974 and now shares hosting duties with his son, Joe Lucia, Jr. Personal attention is one reason Rudi's has remained an "in" restaurant with sophisticates through a succession of owners since it opened 18 years ago.

"About ninety percent of our customers are executives and people who work at big companies, but I think everyone deserves attention, especially women and young people. I like to see young people come in. I come from a family of good cooks, and I really enjoy entertaining," says Lucia. "I think of Rudi's as a festive restaurant. We want you to linger over the food if you like and enjoy the occasion."

Fashion Square
on South Post Oak Road

SAUTEED ARTICHOKES PAULINE

1 (14-ounce) can artichoke hearts, drained
1 cup flour
1 cup milk
1½ cups seasoned bread crumbs
4 tablespoons butter
Juice of half a lemon

1. Dip artichoke hearts in flour, then in milk, then in bread crumbs.
2. Melt butter in skillet. Add artichokes and sauté until golden brown.
3. Pour or squeeze lemon juice over artichokes and heat, stirring gently.

If you like, make your own seasoned bread crumbs using Italian bread, parsley, salt, garlic and an Italian herb blend. Oven-toast with a mixture of olive oil and butter.

CHICKEN EGG-DROP SOUP

1 quart chicken stock
3 eggs
1 cup freshly grated Parmesan cheese
1 tablespoon chopped parsley

1. Bring stock to an even boil in a medium saucepan.
2. In a bowl, mix eggs, cheese and parsley.
3. Whisk egg mixture lightly and quickly into the boiling stock.
4. Cover pan and simmer 12 minutes or cook, stirring, for a few minutes until eggs are set.

Of course homemade chicken stock or consommé is best, but a good quality canned stock may be substituted. It should be well skimmed of fat. In Italian, this egg consommé is called pavese.

PINE NUT SALAD PEARCE

2 heads Boston Bibb lettuce
1 cup salad oil
1 cup red wine vinegar
1 cup water
1 teaspoon dry mustard
1½ teaspoons coarsely ground garlic
½ teaspoon ground pepper
1 cup pine nuts (pignolia)

1. Wash lettuce gently under cold running water or spray. Pat dry.
2. Mix oil with red wine vinegar, water, mustard powder, garlic and pepper in a bowl and chill.
3. Arrange lettuce on four plates.
4. Sprinkle with pine nuts, about ¼ cup per salad, and pour on dressing.

This salad was inspired by Mr. and Mrs. Louis Pearce. They had a similar salad while traveling and asked us to recreate it.

Any light tasting salad oil may be used, but we prefer a good quality imported Italian olive oil.

VEAL LUCERO

½ pound butter
1 pound veal scaloppine cut ¼-inch thick
Flour
Juice of 1 lemon
1 teaspoon chopped parsley
½ pound fresh super lump crab meat

1. Melt ¼ pound butter in a skillet.
2. Dust veal with flour and sauté until lightly brown on both sides. Remove veal from pan and drain on paper towels.
3. Add remaining butter, lemon juice, parsley and crab to skillet; sauté until hot.
4. Place veal on plates and spoon crab meat and sauce over it.

Try to buy Wisconsin milk-fed veal and fresh crab meat in season.

FETTUCCINE ALFREDO

1 pound fettuccine noodles
¼ pound butter
1 cup freshly grated Parmesan cheese
2 cups whipping cream
3 egg yolks

1. Cook fettuccine in boiling salted water in a large pot only until there is a white spot in the center of the pasta (al dente). Drain and rinse immediately with cold water.
2. Melt butter in a large skillet or chafing dish. Add pasta.
3. Stir in cheese and cream and stir, lightly tossing, until pasta is well coated.
4. Stir in egg yolks and heat through.

Cheese, butter and cream should melt into a creamy sauce that coats the noodles. Don't overstir, but be sure pasta is well coated. It is important to use freshly grated Parmesan; that's one secret of fine cooking.

STEAMED FRESH BROCCOLI
(Italian Style)

2 bunches fresh broccoli (about 2 pounds)
½ cup grated Capo Romano cheese
½ cup good quality imported Italian olive oil

1. Wash broccoli and trim. Steam whole in a double boiler over simmering salted water until tender-crisp, about 12 minutes depending on size of broccoli. Remove from pan and arrange on ovenproof tray or plate.
2. Sprinkle with cheese and brush or dribble with oil.
3. Broil until cheese is melted.
4. Serve immediately.

To cook the broccoli, use a steamer pan or covered double boiler which has a steamer rack in it so the broccoli is easy to lift out when it's done. Don't overcook.

The Capo Romano cheese may be hard to find. If so, substitute another hard Romano cheese or freshly grated Parmesan. Romano made from cow's milk is called Vacchino Romano; that made from goat's milk, Caprino Romano.

AMARETTO FREEZE

1 quart homemade-style vanilla ice cream
8 ounces Amaretto liqueur

1. Blend ice cream and Amaretto in blender until creamy.
2. Pour into stemmed glasses or balloon wine glasses and serve.

ruggles restaurant

Dinner for Six

Trout Amandine

Crippen Salad

Veal Kottwitz

D's Cold Buttered Rum

Wine:

With Trout—Schloss Johannisberg
With Veal—Pouilly-Fuissé

Manfred Jachmich, Owner
George Fry, Executive Chef

Trout Almondine

Ruggles reflects the current restaurant trend toward fewer courses and lighter food, and the menu features only ten or so main items. Owner Manfred Jachmich says he is shying away from beef and going more into fish entrées and vegetables because people are eating lighter and are more resistant to higher prices. "At private parties, people are eating smaller portions. We try to give guests a good feel for our food, but we are concentrating on offering a reduced menu with exquisite taste throughout."

The original Ruggles, which opened in 1974, is one of the continuing success stories on Westheimer's restaurant row. In 1979, Jachmich opened Ruggles II in the burgeoning Voss Road area. It has the same Continentally-inspired menu and pleasantly informal atmosphere. Another Ruggles is opening soon in Victoria, Texas.

Jachmich comes from a restaurant family in Koblenz, Germany, and apprenticed in Germany and Switzerland before coming to the U.S. in 1963. He worked for various hotels and restaurants, attended college and later became manager and partner in the Bismarck when it was owned by restaurateur Willie Rometsch. He owned another restaurant, Oliver's, before opening Ruggles.

The casual feeling of New Orleans-style outdoor courtyards and verandas pervades the original Ruggles. The open feeling is achieved with hanging baskets, natural wood and brown latticework and jade green accents. The stained glass windows are from an old English pub. Antiques and provincial country fabrics set the key for the dining room and recently redecorated semi-private rooms. The same fabric gives a rich feeling to the dining areas at Ruggles II where warm brick and paneling create a cozier atmosphere.

903 Westheimer

6540 San Felipe

TROUT AMANDINE

3 filets fresh Gulf trout, skinned and boned
Flour
2 or 3 beaten eggs
Sliced almonds
Butter
Lemon Sauce
Parsley sprigs and lemon wedges for garnish

1. Cut each trout filet into four equal pieces. Wash and pat dry.
2. Dip each piece in flour, then in beaten eggs, then in sliced almonds.
3. Sauté lightly in melted butter until golden.
4. Turn and finish cooking, about 2 minutes.
5. Arrange fish on individual plates and pour the **Lemon Sauce** over filets. Garnish with parsley and a wedge of lemon.

Lemon Sauce

¼ pound butter, melted
1 tablespoon fresh lemon juice
Salt and white pepper
Dash of Worcestershire sauce

1. Mix butter with lemon juice.
2. Add salt, white pepper and Worcestershire sauce to taste.

CRIPPEN SALAD

2 bunches watercress
6 stalks hearts of palm, cut in pieces
Dressing

1. Wash watercress and pat dry.
2. Toss Dressing with watercress and hearts of palm just before serving.

Dressing

¾ cup salad oil
2 tablespoons vinegar
½ teaspoon dry English mustard
Salt and white pepper to taste

Prepare dressing in advance and shake to combine ingredients.

*Watercress is most often used as a garnish, but is very nice as a main
salad ingredient. It gets its name because it grows along streams.
When you buy it, be sure it is a fresh deep green and has crisp stems.
If you store it at home, wash well, shake dry and refrigerate in a tightly
covered container. It may be necessary to wash it several times under
running water to remove all of the sand. It's a good source of vitamins
A and C and iron, if you eat enough.*

VEAL KOTTWITZ

18 medallions of milk fed veal
Salt and white pepper
Flour and butter
3 cups dry white wine
Juice of 1 lemon
12 canned artichoke hearts, cut in quarters
1 pound white mushrooms, sliced

1. Lightly season veal medallions with salt and white pepper. Flour very lightly.
2. Melt butter in a skillet and sauté veal lightly. Set aside and keep warm.
3. In the same skillet, combine wine and lemon juice and simmer gently a few minutes.
4. Add artichoke quarters and mushrooms and cook until mushrooms are tender.
5. Spoon over veal. Top with sauce from the pan.

Good milk fed veal has a grayish-pink color and velvety texture. It should be sautéed quickly. Do not overcook.

D'S COLD BUTTERED RUM

10 scoops butter pecan ice cream (preferably Blue Bell)
9 ounces Myers's rum
3 ounces half-and-half
Cinnamon

1. Make three drinks at a time in a blender by blending 5 scoops ice cream, 3 jiggers rum and 1 jigger half-and-half until thick and creamy.
2. Pour into brandy snifters and garnish with a sprinkle of cinnamon.

 # Tivoli Inn

Dinner for Four

West Coast Salad

Mushroom Soup

Copenhagen Filet

Ofelia Dessert

Wine:

With Salad and Soup—Winkeler Hasensprung Trocken
With Copenhagen Filet—In summer, light French
Beaujolais
In winter, St.-Emilion
With Dessert—German Sekt or California Champagne
After Dinner—Cognac and Demitasse Coffee

Alli Harrigan, Owner
Henri Friis, Chef

The Danes are equally famous for their fine food and their hospitality, and Alli Harrigan has incorporated both in the Tivoli Inn, a small house remodeled in the style of a Danish country inn, color-cued to the red and white of the Danish flag.

The restaurant opened in 1976 and features family recipes for typically Danish fare—roast duck with red cabbage, herring, lox, smorrebrod, liver pâté, frikadeller and seafood with appropriate herbs like caraway, thyme and dill, and sauces. The Danes love sauces, she says.

"This type of cooking is expensive because almost all the food has to be prepared to order. Open-face sandwiches and desserts should be made up as you serve them, and that's the way we do it. The breads are specially baked to our specifications and I grow my own parsley and dill for the restaurant so we can have it all the time." The menu is planned to take advantage of fresh seasonal foods and the availability of traditional ingredients. They are happy to cook special dishes on request, she says.

The atmosphere of cheerful coziness comes from fresh white stuccoed walls, a fireplace, hanging baskets, fresh flowers on tables dressed with red skirts and white overcloths, antique copper etchings, paintings, posters of the Tivoli Gardens and the pleasant diversion of piano music in the evening.

"I come from a family that is interested in cooking and that loves to have parties. Several members of the family assist in the restaurant, so I feel I am entertaining people in my home when they come to the Tivoli."

715 Hawthorne

WEST COAST SALAD

1 cup frozen or fresh peas and carrots
1 head Boston lettuce or 1 small head iceberg lettuce
1 cup cooked shrimp
½ cup Alaska King crab meat
1 cup waterpacked Danish mussels, drained
Black lumpfish (Limfjord) caviar
Tomato and lemon wedges for garnish
Dill Mayonnaise Sauce

1. Cook peas and carrots al dente (tender-crisp) and chill.
2. Remove outer leaves of lettuce and reserve for decoration. Quarter the
   lettuce and cut or tear into small pieces in large bowl.
3. Add chilled peas and carrots to lettuce.
4. Add shrimp, crab and mussels and toss lightly.
5. Arrange outer leaves of lettuce on a tray and top with salad mixture.
   Sprinkle with caviar.
6. Garnish tray with tomato and lemon wedges and serve with
   Dill Mayonnaise Sauce to be added at the table.

Dill Mayonnaise Sauce

½ cup mayonnaise
½ cup whipped cream
¼ teaspoon white pepper
¼ teaspoon salt
½ teaspoon dried dill weed or 1½ teaspoons fresh dill

1. Fold whipped cream into mayonnaise.
2. Add seasonings and chill thoroughly.

Fresh cut dill may be added to the salad mixture; it gives the seafood a very special flavor. Most Scandinavians couldn't cook without dill. A variation of this sauce is a thick homemade-style mayonnaise and dill weed thinned with St. Peter Liebfraumilch wine. It is a lighter and more delicate sauce than the above and is delicious with smoked salmon as an appetizer.

Add any other shellfish of your choice. Feel free to experiment. I have had this first course many times in Denmark, Sweden and Norway, and each salad has been just a little different. The sauce is "the dot over the i."

MUSHROOM SOUP

½ pound fresh white mushrooms, thinly sliced
4 tablespoons sweet butter
1 (16-ounce) can beef broth or homemade beef broth
Salt and freshly ground black pepper
4 ounces half and half

1. Lightly sauté mushrooms in butter.
2. Add broth and bring to a light boil. Add salt and pepper (go a little heavy on the pepper).
3. Reduce heat and stir in half and half.
4. Serve with your favorite bread.

The most important tip is to choose fresh white closed mushrooms. This soup is light and is just as good reheated the next day if you have leftovers. For a luncheon, have a cup of mushroom soup and small Danish open faced sandwiches, smorrebrod, *and just let your imagination run wild from roast beef with fried onions and remoulade sauce to ham with a garnish of pea and carrot salad. The decorations on open face sandwiches are unlimited. Just use whatever you have at hand and each little sandwich becomes a masterpiece that is hard to resist. Using leftovers, you can create a tray full of marvels at very low cost.*

COPENHAGEN FILET

1 whole pork tenderloin (about 1 to 1½ pounds)
4 tablespoons butter
1 large yellow onion, thinly sliced
1 large green pepper, thinly sliced
2 ounces white mushrooms, thinly sliced
1 cup canned tomatoes, diced (or fresh ripe tomatoes or small cherry
    tomatoes, cut in half)

1. Remove fat, tendons and silk skin from meat. Slice in 1-inch thick pieces
   and pound out gently. Set aside.
2. In a skillet, sauté onion and green pepper in butter, then add mushrooms
   and tomatoes and simmer gently until done. Remove from heat.
3. Sauté meat in a little butter and season to taste with salt and pepper.
4. Place meat on large hot platter and arrange the vegetable mixture across
   the top. Serve immediately.

*This entrée may be served with potato croquettes or a similar dish, but
hot French bread or rolls would also be suitable.*

*Pork tenderloin does not reheat well, but it can be a delight cold. Start with
a piece of lettuce (Boston is my favorite). Arrange thin slices of cold pork
tenderloin on top and garnish with a slice of cucumber and tomato wedges
or thin slices of pickled beets and raw or cooked apples.*

OFELIA DESSERT

Vanilla ice cream
Peter Heering liqueur
Whipped cream
Chopped walnuts
Grated dark sweet chocolate

1. On individual dishes, arrange a scoop of your favorite vanilla ice cream.
2. Pour a jigger of Peter Heering over it.
3. Garnish with a big flourish of whipped cream, chopped nuts and grated
   chocolate.

*This complete dinner lends itself quite well to our warm weather, summer or
winter. Desserts need not be a chore. After a large dinner, a small eye-appealing
dessert of ice cream takes only minutes to put together.*

Dinner for Six

Carpaccio Tony's

Capellini with Basil

Veal Steaks with Green Peppercorns

Frittata

Strawberry-Raspberry Soufflé

Wine:

*With Carpaccio and Capellini—Puligny-Montrachet
1977 or '78
With Veal—Château Peymartin 1973
With Soufflé—Trockenbeerenauslese*

Tony Vallone, Owner
Frank Garza, Chef

Tony's has evolved from Italian to Continental to French in character. Today the product of the kitchen is a blend of haute cuisine, nouvelle cuisine and American regional cooking, with a slight Mediterranean touch. Vallone strives for a total fine dining experience, including a thoughtful orchestration of food, wine, service, decor and timing presented with panache. Tony's attracts Houston's status clientele and their guests, visiting notables and food and wine connoisseurs.

"I think the whole thing to cooking is a delicate touch. So many restaurants overpower the food. You have to use the finest, freshest ingredients and give each dish its own personality and originality. We constantly try to come up with new ideas. We cater to our clientele—people who know and care about food—with cooked-to-order specialties. Not many of our regular customers even order from the menu; they ask their captain."

Tony's now has an in-house florist, and innovative arrangements of fresh flowers help create serene retreats that echo the colors of paintings and Chinese porcelains from Tony's personal collection.

The wines, which Tony collects as a passion, total about 110,000 bottles, and the wine cellar is the scene of some of the city's most elegant, intimate private parties.

Among the dishes that have earned Tony's recognition as a Mobil Four Star restaurant, *Playboy* magazine's Critic's Choice and the coveted *Holiday* Awards are Lobster Bisque, fresh fish dishes such as Red Snapper Grenobloise, hot dessert soufflés and Carpaccio—paperthin slices of raw beef tenderloin with a hot mustard sauce. The latter was singled out for comment at a recent Chaine des Rotisseurs dinner.

1801 South Post Oak

CARPACCIO TONY'S

1 pound very lean, highest quality raw beef tenderloin
1 egg yolk
2 teaspoons Dijon mustard
Seasoned salt and freshly ground pepper
2 tablespoons fresh lemon juice
1 cup Italian olive oil
2 tablespoons finely chopped shallots
1 tablespoon Worcestershire sauce (optional)
Liquid hot pepper sauce
1 tablespoon finely chopped capers
½ cup rich beef stock

1. Place beef in freezer until firm and about half frozen. Slice as thinly as possible. Refrigerate until needed.
2. Make mayonnaise by preferred method, or: place egg yolk in mixing bowl and add mustard, salt and pepper to taste. Add lemon juice. Start beating with a wire whisk or electric mixer and gradually add oil, bit by bit, until sauce begins to thicken, beating constantly. As mixture thickens, the oil may be added a little faster.
3. Place shallots in cheesecloth and run under cold water. Squeeze to extract as much moisture as possible. Add shallots to the mayonnaise.
4. To make the sauce: stir Worcestershire, a dash of pepper sauce, capers and beef stock into mayonnaise. Makes a little over 1 cup.
5. Arrange overlapping slices of beef on plates and top with a spoonful of the sauce.

The meat must be of the highest quality and must be fresh. It should be very cold and partially frozen. If completely frozen, it will become mushy and unpalatable in texture.

CAPELLINI WITH BASIL

2 cups dry white wine
1 cup chopped shallots
2 cups heavy (whipping) cream
Seasoning salt and pepper to taste
1½ cups tomato paste
2 tablespoons chopped garlic
2 cups chopped fresh basil
1 pound capellini pasta

1. Combine wine and shallots in a saucepan over high heat. Reduce until wine is completely evaporated.
2. Lower heat and add cream. Cook until mixture comes to a boil. Remove pan from heat, add salt and pepper to taste and whisk in tomato paste. Return to heat and cook until mixture comes to a boil.
3. Add garlic and a minute later, the fresh basil.
4. Boil capellini al dente and serve immediately, covered with sauce.

VEAL STEAKS WITH GREEN PEPPERCORNS

4 (½ pound) veal steaks
3 tablespoons green peppercorns
3 tablespoons olive oil
4 tablespoons butter
⅓ cup finely chopped shallots
1 cup Madeira or dry red wine
1 cup heavy (whipping) cream

1. Pound the veal steaks lightly with a flat mallet.
2. Drain the peppercorns and rinse under cold running water. Crush about a third of them and press into both sides of each steak. Sprinkle with salt.
3. Heat the oil and 1 tablespoon of the butter in a large, heavy skillet and add the veal. Cook over medium high heat about 2 minutes or until nicely browned on one side.
4. Turn the steaks and cook 2 to 3 minutes longer. Remove the meat and keep it warm.
5. Pour off the fat from the skillet and add a tablespoon of butter and the shallots. Cook briefly, stirring, and add the wine. Cook over high heat, stirring, until most of the wine is reduced, 5 to 10 minutes.
6. Stir in the cream. Boil vigorously about 2 minutes and add any liquid that has accumulated around the veal steaks. Add the remaining peppercorns, more or less, to taste. Simmer about 5 minutes and swirl in the remaining butter.
7. Slice the steak diagonally and spoon the sauce over it.

FRITTATA (Italian Vegetable Pie)

1 cup chopped cooked asparagus or broccoli
1 cup chopped zucchini
1 cup cooked chopped spinach, drained
1 cup chopped large marinated hearts of artichoke
½ cup chopped onion
Olive oil
1 clove garlic
Seasoning salt
Black pepper
Oregano
8 eggs
3 tablespoons freshly grated Parmesan cheese

1. Combine vegetables with some olive oil and chopped garlic in an ovenproof skillet and season with salt, pepper and oregano. Sauté about 4 to 5 minutes, stirring constantly.
2. Beat eggs with Parmesan. Stir in sautéed vegetables, then return mixture to skillet.
3. Cover and cook over low heat until lightly browned on the bottom. Place in 350-degree oven and bake 10 minutes or until nicely browned.
4. Loosen the omelet by sliding a small spatula around the edges. Serve in wedges.

STRAWBERRY-RASPBERRY SOUFFLE

2 cups sliced ripe strawberries
Sugar
2 tablespoons red currant jelly
3 tablespoons butter
3 tablespoons flour
½ cup milk
4 egg yolks, beaten
1 cup raspberry purée (fresh or frozen)
5 egg whites
½ teaspoon cream of tartar

1. Preheat oven to 350 degrees.
2. Place strawberries in a dish and sprinkle with a little sugar. Beat currant jelly and pour over them.
3. In the top part of a double boiler, melt the butter over boiling water. Stir in the flour. Cook a few minutes, then stir in the milk. Cook about 5 minutes, stirring constantly, until all is blended into a smooth sauce.
4. Remove top of double boiler from heat and let cool.
5. Add beaten egg yolks and stir until the mixture is smooth.
6. Add the puréed raspberries. Sweeten with 1 tablespoon sugar, if necessary. Set aside to cool about 15 minutes.
7. Beat the egg whites. Sprinkle in the cream of tartar while beating and beat until stiff, but not dry.
8. Add a little of the egg whites to the raspberry sauce. Return mixture to remaining egg whites, lifting and folding gently until just blended.
9. Heat the sliced strawberries and place in the bottom of a buttered sugared 2-quart soufflé dish. Pour the raspberry sauce over. Bake in preheated oven about 25 minutes, until well puffed.

In making soufflés, it is very important to incorporate the egg whites properly. They should be added to the sauce mixture when it is cool. Do not overmix or egg whites will break down. Fold a small amount into the cooked mixture first, then fold into the remaining beaten egg whites. Do not beat or stir vigorously, just fold in gently.

Uncle Tai's 湘園

Dinner for Six

Uncle Tai's Special Drink

Crispy Walnuts

Special Hunan Vegetable Pie

Shredded Pork and Pickled Vegetable Soup

Uncle Tai's Beef

Uncle Tai's Shrimp

Sesame Bananas

Wine:
Wan Fu or other dry white wine or
Tsingtao Chinese Beer

Wen Dah Tai, Owner-Chef

Wen Dah (Uncle) Tai, who moved from New York and opened Uncle Tai's Hunan Yuan in June, 1979, may be a newcomer to Houston, but he predicted correctly that the spicy cuisine of his homeland would be successful in the land of Tex-Mex where everybody loves a jalapeño. The slick lacquer-black menus are peppered with asterisks that identify the hot and spicy dishes, as well as dishes that Uncle Tai says are being served for the first time in Houston. Spiciness and the use of monosodium glutamate will be adjusted on request.

Decor of the Galleria-area restaurant is sophisticated and fashionably elegant—neutral beige backgrounds punctuated by handsome cinnabar lacquer screens and paneling. One wall is covered with a photomural done by a 92-year-old Chinese artist who came from Taiwan to supervise its installation.

Uncle is a title of respect in his native country, Tai says. When he decided to move to Houston, he brought his wife, four sons and a veritable commune of chefs and kitchen help with him. Many menu items take their names from scenic wonders of his homeland, such as Lake Tung Ting Shrimp. "Hunan is one of the central provinces of mainland China and offers some of the most beautiful scenery in Asia," he says through an interpreter. "The hardy people of the Hunan area developed the unique and spicy cuisine to satisfy their appetites as well as to warm them during the long cold months. The hot food also pleases the body in hot, humid climates." Among the dishes he has introduced to Houston are the Special Hunan Vegetable Pie, a unique vegetable combination layered with bean curd skin sheets like Chinese puff pastry, and the Yunnan Steamer Pot, a meal cooked in a steamer pot, which must be ordered in advance.

Uncle Tai desires that his customers understand the foods he serves, so he and his staff conduct free cooking classes on Sunday afternoons, by reservation.

1980 S. Post Oak in Two Post Oak Central

UNCLE TAI'S SPECIAL DRINK

Per serving:

1 jigger dark rum
1 jigger light rum
1 jigger apricot brandy
1 teaspoon Orgeat almond syrup
2 dashes Triple Sec
Orange juice
Pineapple juice

1. Combine rums, apricot brandy, almond syrup and Triple Sec.
2. Fill glass with equal portions orange juice and pineapple juice.

Orgeat almond syrup is a flavored sugar syrup which is available at liquor stores. At Uncle Tai's, the drinks are decorated with miniature paper parasols.

CRISPY WALNUTS

1 pound walnuts, shelled, peeled and halved
¼ teaspoon salt
3 cups sugar
½ cup honey
5 cups oil

1. Wash walnuts thoroughly. Fill a wok with water about half way and put the walnuts in. Bring to a boil and let them boil about 3 minutes. Drain and wash them again.
2. Pour 4 cups water into the wok. Add salt, sugar and honey.
3. Return walnuts to the wok and cook about 15 minutes or until liquid begins to thicken. When thickened, pour the contents into a large bowl and let them soak 24 hours.
4. Remove walnuts from the sugar water and drain in a strainer.
5. Heat oil in wok to 350 degrees and add walnuts. Stir occasionally until walnuts turn golden brown.
6. Remove from wok and spread out to cool.
7. When cold, store in airtight container or jar to maintain crispness.

These are one of the most popular items on Uncle Tai's menu. Delicious served as an appetizer with drinks.

SPECIAL HUNAN VEGETABLE PIE

3 pieces bean curd skin sheets (dried bean curd)
10 small dried shrimp
2 large, dried, black Chinese mushrooms
1 (1-inch) piece fresh ginger root
2 scallions
Oil
1 winter bamboo shoot
1½ tablespoons soy sauce
1 tablespoon dry sherry
1 teaspoon sugar
1 teaspoon flavor enhancer (optional)
Black pepper
2 cups chicken stock
2 eggs
Water
1 cup all-purpose flour
1 recipe **Pancakes**
1 recipe **Sauce**
Scallion Brushes
Parsley and decoratively cut radishes for garnish

1. Using wet, hot towels, moisten the bean curd skin sheets and set
   aside until ready to use. Cover with hot towels to retain the
   moisture.
2. In separate small bowls, cover the dried shrimp and mushrooms
   with a little boiling water. When soft, drain and mince finely
   with a knife or cleaver. Mince the ginger. Finely chop scallions.
3. In 1 tablespoon oil, stir-fry the minced shrimp, mushrooms
   and bamboo shoot, adding 1 tablespoon of the soy sauce, the
   sherry, sugar, flavor enhancer and black pepper to taste. After a
   minute, when most of the liquid has evaporated, stir in the
   scallions and remove the filling to a container to cool.
4. In a large, flat, rectangular pan, combine chicken stock and
   remaining soy sauce.
5. Dip a softened bean curd sheet into stock mixture and lay out
   flat on a work surface. Sprinkle lightly with filling. Repeat
   dipping process with a second bean curd sheet, laying it on top
   of the first and sprinkling with a little of the filling. Cover with
   a third sheet which has been dipped in the stock, but do not
   sprinkle with filling.

6. Make sure all the corners of the bean curd skin package are thoroughly moistened and gently fold into a 7x5-inch shape. Set aside.

7. Make a batter by combining the eggs with a little water and beating. Stirring vigorously, pour the egg mixture into the flour. The resulting batter should have the consistency of heavy cream. Add more water if necessary.

8. Heat oil for deep-frying in a wok to 300 degrees. Moisten the whole pie with the egg batter and gently slip it into the hot oil. Increase the heat and cook, turning occasionally and gently, until the pie is golden brown on both sides. The pie may form pockets of air in the center and puff up. If this happens while you are cooking it, prick them with the point of a sharp pin.

9. Drain well and cut into 8 to 10 rectangular pieces. Serve wrapped in a **Pancake** with **Sauce** and a **Scallion Brush** and garnish with parsley and decorative radishes.

Pancakes

2 cups sifted all-purpose flour
¾ cup boiling water
2 tablespoons sesame or cooking oil

1. Pour the boiling water into the flour and mix well with chopsticks. Gather the dough into a ball and on a well-floured surface, knead about 10 minutes until dough is smooth and satiny. Set aside, cover with a damp cloth and let rest about 15 minutes.

2. After resting, roll the dough into a cylindrical shape about 1½ inches in diameter. Cut crosswise into 12 rounds.

3. Lightly brush some oil on one side of each piece and place two pieces together with the oiled sides together, resembling a little sandwich. Roll each sandwich into a 6 to 7-inch circle.

4. Cook the dough circles one at a time on an ungreased skillet over low heat 1 minute, then turn over. When very lightly browned, remove from heat and carefully separate into individual pancakes. Serve immediately or reheat by steaming them over a small quantity of water.

Sauce

½ cup hoisin sauce
1 tablespoon sesame oil
1 tablespoon sugar
1 teaspoon sherry

Combine all ingredients and serve as a sauce for the vegetable pie
or for Peking duck.

Scallion Brushes

1 bunch scallions
Ice water

1. Trim off the root ends of scallions. Cut 2 to 3-inch pieces
   off the lower white end of scallions. Reserve the upper green
   parts for some other purpose.
2. Using the point of a small, thin, sharp knife, score the white ends
   of the scallions in 1-inch cuts, cutting away from the greens.
   Evenly space 5 to 8 such cuts around the circumference of each
   stalk, so that the scallion ends may open out.
3. When cut, drop in ice water until the ends curl.

SHREDDED PORK AND PICKLED VEGETABLE SOUP

4 ounces boneless fresh pork, cut from the ham or fileted from the
    rib section of the loin, in the shape of a block 2 inches long
1 piece Szechuan pickled vegetable, the size of an egg
½ bamboo shoot
4 snow peas
1 quart water
3 cups chicken stock
½ teaspoon salt
½ teaspoon flavor enhancer (optional)

1. Slice semi-frozen pork with the grain into pieces ⅙-inch thick
   and 2 inches long. Neatly stack the slices in an overlapping row,
   making sure that the grain of each slice is parallel to the grain
   of its adjacent slices. Still cutting with the grain, cut pork into
   shreds ⅙-inch wide.
2. Wash the pickled vegetable under cold running water, taking care
   to remove all of the pickling material. Cut it into thin slices
   ⅙-inch thick, then cut the slices into shreds ⅙-inch wide.
3. Rinse bamboo shoot under cold running water. Cut it into thin
   lengthwise slices ½-inch thick. Cut slices into shreds ⅙-inch thick.
4. Rinse and pull strings from ends of snow peas. Cut lengthwise
   into fine shreds.
5. Heat 1 quart water in a wok or heavy saucepan until it is at a full
   rolling boil. Add all the pork shreds at once and stir with chopsticks until they separate from each other and change color from
   pink to gray. As soon as water returns to the boil, drain immediately.
   Do not overcook or meat will toughen. Discard water.
6. Return the same wok to highest heat and add chicken stock. When
   it boils, add the pickled vegetable and bamboo shoot, salt and
   (optional) flavor enhancer. Return soup to boil and cook 1
   minute. Taste for seasoning (you may need more salt), then add
   the pork shreds and snow peas. Cook 15 to 30 seconds longer, just
   until the soup returns to boil.
7. Spoon away any scum which may have floated to the surface and
   serve immediately.

*Note: To shred pork: At least six hours before serving, freeze. Remove
from freezer about one hour before you're ready to use it so when you
slice it, it is still semi-frozen. Use of a 12 or 14-inch wok is recommended.*

Pickled vegetable is available at Chinese food specialty shops.

UNCLE TAI'S BEEF

1½ pounds flank steak
⅔ cup plus 3 tablespoons water
½ teaspoon baking soda
¼ teaspoon salt
3 tablespoons dry sherry
1 egg white
3½ tablespoons cornstarch
4 cups plus 2 tablespoons peanut oil
2 scallions, cut in half-inch lengths (about ⅓ cup)
3 tablespoons dried orange peel
3 thin slices fresh ginger, cut in half-inch cubes
1 long, thin, fresh hot red pepper, chopped (optional)
3 tablespoons soy sauce
¼ teaspoon flavor enhancer (optional)
2 tablespoons sugar
1 teaspoon sesame oil
¼ cup chicken broth
10 dried, small, hot red pepper pods

1. Place steak on a flat surface. Holding a sharp knife parallel to the beef, slice it in half width-wise. Cut each half into very thin strips, about ¼-inch. There should be about 4 cups loosely packed strips.
2. Place beef in a mixing bowl and add ⅔ cup water blended with the soda. Refrigerate at least one hour, preferably overnight. When ready to cook, rinse beef thoroughly under cold running water. Drain thoroughly and pat dry.
3. Add salt, 1 tablespoon sherry and egg white and stir until the egg white is bubbly. Add 1½ tablespoons cornstarch and 2 tablespoons oil. Stir to blend.
4. Combine the scallions, dried orange peel, fresh ginger and fresh red pepper. Set aside.
5. Combine the remaining 2 tablespoons wine, soy sauce, (optional) flavor enhancer, sugar, remaining 2 tablespoons cornstarch blended with remaining 3 tablespoons water, sesame oil and chicken broth. Stir to blend.
6. Heat remaining 4 cups oil in a wok or skillet and when it is almost smoking, add the beef. Cook about 45 seconds, stirring constantly. Scoop it out. Drain meat well, leaving oil in the wok continuously heating. Return meat to wok and cook over high

heat 15 seconds, stirring. Drain again. Return meat a third time to the hot oil and cook, stirring. Drain the meat.

7. Drain wok completely. Return 2 tablespoons of the oil to the wok and add hot pepper pods.
8. Stir peppers over high heat until brown and almost blackened, about 30 seconds. Remove. Add scallion mixture and stir.
9. Add beef and cook, stirring constantly, about 10 seconds.
10. Add sherry mixture, stirring, and cook about 15 seconds until hot and meat is well coated.

Dried orange peel is available in Oriental food shops and import stores. To make at home, peel an orange (eliminate as much of the pulp as possible), cut into strips, place on a baking sheet and bake in 200-degree oven until dried. Store in a tightly covered container.

The purpose of cooking the meat three times in the oil is to make the meat crisp on the outside but retain its juiciness within.

UNCLE TAI'S SHRIMP

10 giant shrimp
4½ tablespoons dry sherry or shao hsing wine
2 egg whites
4 cups plus 1½ tablespoons peanut oil
½ teaspoon salt
2½ tablespoons cornstarch
2 scallions, white part only, trimmed and shredded
5 thin slices fresh ginger, shredded
2 tablespoons water
2 tablespoons soy sauce
2½ tablespoons white vinegar
2 tablespoons sugar
½ teaspoon sesame oil
⅓ cup chicken broth
½ cup loosely packed cilantro

1. Peel shrimp, split in half and rinse to devein. Pat dry.
2. Place shrimp in bowl and add 1½ tablespoons sherry, egg whites and 1½ tablespoons oil. Stir until whites become bubbly.
3. Add half the salt and 1½ tablespoons cornstarch. Stir to blend.
4. Prepare scallions and ginger and set aside.
5. Combine remaining 3 tablespoons sherry, remaining tablespoon cornstarch blended with water, soy sauce, vinegar, sugar, remaining salt, sesame oil and broth.
6. Heat remaining 4 cups oil in a wok or skillet and add shrimp, one at a time. Cook about 1 minute, then scoop out, leaving the oil in the wok continuously heating. Return shrimp to oil and cook about 30 seconds. Drain wok completely.
7. Return about 1 tablespoon oil to the wok and add scallions and ginger, stirring constantly. Cook about 5 seconds.
8. Add shrimp and vinegar mixture. Toss and stir-fry until piping hot and shrimp is coated evenly. Garnish with cilantro.

Cilantro is fresh coriander leaves and is sometimes called Chinese parsley. It is available in Chinese and Mexican markets and in some supermarkets in the produce section.

SESAME BANANAS

½ cup raw white sesame seeds
½ cup sugar
1 cup flour
Water
1 tablespoon baking powder
2 bananas
½ cup cornstarch
4 cups vegetable oil

1. Sauté sesame seeds (dry with no oil) to a golden color. Put in blender and process to a powder-like texture. Mix with sugar. (This makes Sesame Sugar.)
2. Mix flour with enough water to make a batter-like consistency; it should not be too thin. Add baking powder and mix again.
3. Remove banana peels and slice bananas diagonally about 1½ inches apart. Roll in cornstarch.
4. Heat oil to about 300 degrees.
5. Dip banana pieces into batter, then into hot oil. Remove when they turn a light golden brown.
6. Put on a plate and sprinkle with Sesame Sugar. Serve.

Rolling the bananas in cornstarch helps keep the flour on the banana when cooking.

APPETIZERS

Avocado with Baby Shrimp (Rotisserie for
    Beef and Bird) — 125
Capellini Siciliana (D'Amico's) — 46
Capellini with Basil (Tony's) — 154
Carpaccio Tony's (Tony's) — 153
Crab Claws Lamonte (Nino's) — 103
Crawfish Etouffée in Pastry Shells (Brennan's) — 3
Crispy Walnuts (Uncle Tai's) — 161
Fritto di Mozzarella (D'Amico's) — 45
Hickory Smoked Shrimp (Confederate House) — 37
Liptauer Cheese (La Quiche) — 80
Liver Pâté (La Quiche) — 79
Oysters à l'Ancienne (Che) — 19
Oysters Bourguignon (Charley's 517) — 13
Paper-Wrapped Fried Chicken (China Garden) — 28
Queso a la Parrilla (Ninfa's) — 95
Sautéed Artichokes Pauline (Rudi's) — 133
Shrimp Foulard's (Foulard's) — 55
Special Hunan Vegetable Pie (Uncle Tai's) — 162
Spiedini di Gamberi dell' Adreatico (D'Amico's) — 48
Stuffed Artichokes with Crabmeat, General
    Louis Pulaski (Maxim's) — 89
Trout Amandine (Ruggles) — 141

BEVERAGES

Amaretto Freeze (Rudi's) — 137
Brandy Freeze (Maxim's) — 91
Café Brûlot (Brennan's) — 9
Caffè d'Amico (D'Amico's) — 51
D's Cold Buttered Rum (Ruggles) — 143
Flaming Café Amaretto (Hugo's Window Box) — 75
Pedernales Fruit Shake (Good Eats Cafe) — 65
Strawberry Daiquiri (La Quiche) — 79
Uncle Tai's Special Drink (Uncle Tai's) — 161

BREADS

Cheddar Cheese Bread (La Quiche) — 84
Hush Puppies (Confederate House) — 40

Southern Style Jalapeño Corn Bread Muffins
   (Good Eats Cafe)   68
Yeast Rolls (Rotisserie for Beef and Bird)   128

DESSERTS & DESSERT ACCENTS

Amaretto Freeze (Rudi's)   137
Brandy Freeze (Maxim's)   91
Bread Pudding with Hot Whiskey Sauce
   (Rotisserie for Beef and Bird)   128
Confederate Pie (Confederate House)   41
Cream Cheese Frosting (La Quiche)   85
Crêpes Del Carmen (Foulard's)   61
Crêpes Fitzgerald (Brennan's)   8
D'Amico's Chocolate Cheesecake (D'Amico's)   50
D's Cold Buttered Rum (Ruggles)   143
Flan (Ninfa's)   99
Grand Marnier Ice Parfait (Rivoli)   121
Hot Whiskey Sauce (Rotisserie for
   Beef and Bird)   129
La Quiche Carrot Cake (La Quiche)   85
Ofelia Dessert (Tivoli Inn)   149
Peanut Butter Pie (Good Eats Cafe)   69
Savarin (Hugo's Window Box)   75
Sesame Bananas (Uncle Tai's)   169
Sfingis (Nino's)   107
Strawberry-Raspberry Soufflé (Tony's)   157
Swedish Cream with Fresh Raspberries (Charley's 517)   15
Walnut Pie (Rainbow Lodge)   115
Walnut Torte (Che)   23

ENTREES

Beef Bourguignon (Maxim's)   91
Beef Steak alla Nino (Nino's)   106
Beer Batter Fried Trout (Confederate House)   38
Carnitas with Green Sauce, Red Sauce and
   Guacamole (Ninfa's)   97
Chicken Marsala (La Quiche)   83
Copenhagen Filet (Tivoli Inn)   149
Filet Mignon Debris (Brennan's)   5

Fresh Gulf Trout in Brown Butter Sauce
   (Rainbow Lodge)   113
Lamb Loin Beauharnaise (Che)   20
Petti di Pollo Fiorentina (D'Amico's)   49
Pheasant Sautéed (Foulard's)   59
Poached Filet of Salmon, Clarice (Foulard's)   56
Red Snapper Pontchartrain (Charley's 517)   14
Roast Duckling à l'Orange (Rotisserie for
   Beef and Bird)   126
Savannah-Style Beer-Batter Fried Chicken
   (Good Eats Cafe)   66
Seafood Gumbo (La Quiche)   81
Stir-Fried Beef with Oyster Sauce (China Garden)   30
Stir-Fried Chicken with Walnuts (China Garden)   31
Stir-Fried Shrimp with Garlic (China Garden)   29
Stuffed Dover Sole Zielinsky (Rivoli)   120
Uncle Tai's Beef (Uncle Tai's)   166
Uncle Tai's Shrimp (Uncle Tai's)   168
Veal Citron (Hugo's Window Box)   74
Veal Kottwitz (Ruggles)   143
Veal Lucero (Rudi's)   135
Veal Steaks with Peppercorns (Tony's)   155

SALAD DRESSINGS

French Dressing (Maxim's)   90
Dressing (Rivoli)   119
Dressing (Ruggles)   142
Dill Mayonnaise Sauce (Tivoli)   147

SALADS

Boston Butter Lettuce Salad (Hugo's Window Box)   74
Chatelaine Salad (Brennan's)   4
Crippen Salad (Ruggles)   142
Insalata di Arancia (D'Amico's)   47
La Quiche Spinach Salad (La Quiche)   82
Marinated Vegetables (Rainbow Lodge)   112
Pine Nut Salad Pearce (Rudi's)   134
Poireaux Salad (Che)   22
Rainbow Salad (Rainbow Lodge)   111
Ratatouille (Rainbow Lodge)   111

Schlumberger Salad (Maxim's)   90
Spinach and Watercress Salad with Pine Nuts
    (Rivoli)   119
Tabouli (Rainbow Lodge)   112
West Coast Salad (Tivoli Inn)   147
Wilhelmina Salad (Confederate House)   37

SAUCES AND SPECIAL SEASONINGS

Béarnaise Sauce (Che)   22
Beef Brown Sauce (Brennan's)   7
Beef Stock (Brennan's)   6
Beurre Manié (Hugo's Window Box)   73
Brown Butter Sauce (Rainbow Lodge)   114
Brown Sauce (Che)   21
Confederate House Tartar Sauce (Confederate House)   38
Guacamole (Ninfa's)   98
Hollandaise (Foulard's)   57
Hollandaise (Rainbow Lodge)   114
Lemon Sauce (Ruggles)   141
Ninfa's Green Sauce (Ninfa's)   97
Ninfa's Red Sauce (Ninfa's)   98
Orange Sauce (Rotisserie for Beef and Bird)   127
Sauce (Uncle Tai's)   164
Sauce Madere (Che)   21
Sauce Marinara (D'Amico's)   45
Sawmill Gravy (Good Eats Cafe)   66
Stuffing (Rivoli)   120
Tarragon Butter (Che)   21
White Sauce (D'Amico's)   50

SOUPS

Champignons de Paris (Che)   19
Chicken Egg-Drop Soup (Rudi's)   134
Chilled Cream of Avocado (Foulard's)   55
Cream of Cucumber Soup (Rainbow Lodge)   113
Cream of Spinach Soup (Brennan's)   4
Gazpacho (Rivoli)   119
Hot and Sour Soup (China Garden)   27
Minestrone with Miniature Meatballs (Nino's)   105

Mushroom Soup (Tivoli Inn) 148
Onion Soup Gratinée with Calvados (Rotisserie
    for Beef and Bird) 125
Oyster Velouté (Hugo's Window Box) 73
Seafood Gumbo (La Quiche) 81
Shredded Pork and Pickled Vegetable Soup
    (Uncle Tai's) 165
Sopa de Tortilla (Ninfa's) 96
Vichyssoise with Walnuts (Charley's 517) 13

VEGETABLES AND SIDE DISHES

Carrots Lyonnaise (Charley's 517) 15
Country Squash Casserole (Good Eats Cafe) 67
Fettuccine Alfredo (Rudi's) 136
Fresh Asparagus with Hollandaise (Rainbow Lodge) 114
Fresh Okra and Tomatoes (Good Eats Cafe) 68
Fried Zucchini and Cauliflower (Nino's) 104
Frittata (Tony's) 156
Pancakes (Uncle Tai's) 163
Pomme Macaire (Foulard's) 60
Sautéed Asparagus (Foulard's) 60
Sautéed Mushrooms (Confederate House) 39
Scallion Brushes (Uncle Tai's) 164
Steamed Fresh Broccoli (Rudi's) 136
Stir-Fried Vegetarian Dish (China Garden) 32
Strawberry Sorbet (Foulard's) 58
Yellow Squash (Rainbow Lodge) 115
Zucchini Casserole with Sour Cream (Rotisserie
    for Beef and Bird) 127

notes

notes

DINING IN—THE GREAT CITIES

A Collection of Gourmet Recipes from the Finest Chefs in the Country

If you enjoyed Dining In—Houston, Vol. II, the following cookbook/restaurant guides are now available:

_____ Feasting In—Atlanta	_____ Dining In—Milwaukee
_____ Dining In—Baltimore	_____ Dining In—Minneapolis/St. Paul
_____ Dining In—Boston	_____ Dining In—Monterey Peninsula
_____ Dining In—Chicago	_____ Feasting In—New Orleans
_____ Dining In—Dallas	_____ Dining In—Pittsburgh
_____ Dining In—Denver	_____ Dining In—Portland
_____ Dining In—Hawaii	_____ Dining In—San Francisco
_____ Dining In—Houston, Vol I	_____ Dining In—Seattle, Vol II
_____ Dining In—Houston, Vol II	_____ Dining In—St. Louis
_____ Dining In—Kansas City	_____ Dining In—Toronto
_____ Dining In—Los Angeles	_____ Dining In—Vancouver

Forthcoming Titles:

Dining In—Cleveland   Dining In—Sun Valley
Dining In—Philadelphia   Dining In—Washington, D:C.
Dining In—Phoenix

To order, send $7.95 plus $1.00 postage and handling per book.

> ☐   CHECK HERE IF YOU WOULD LIKE TO HAVE A
> DIFFERENT **DINING IN**— COOKBOOK SENT TO YOU
> ONCE A MONTH.
> Payable by Mastercard, Visa or COD. Returnable if not satisfied.
> $7.95 plus $1.00 postage and handling for each book.

. . . .

BILL TO:

Name _____

Address _____

City _____ State _____ Zip _____

☐ Payment enclosed   ☐ Send COD

☐ Charge

Visa # _____

Exp. Date _____

Mastercard # _____

Exp. Date _____

Signature _____

SHIP TO:

Name _____

Address _____

City _____ State _____ Zip _____

. . . .

Name _____

Address _____

City _____ State _____ Zip _____

. . . .

Name _____

Address _____

City _____ State _____ Zip _____

PEANUT BUTTER PUBLISHING

Peanut Butter Towers · 2733 4th Avenue South · Seattle, WA 98134